EGYPT

1632

EGYPT

EGYPT

J. J. AUGUSTIN PUBLISHER NEW YORK

PHOTOGRAPHED BY
HOYNINGEN-HUENE

TEXT BY
GEORGE STEINDORFF

This book was set in 14 pt. Bodoni Linotype
printed and bound by
the George Grady Press, New York

Jacket design by Alexis Brodovitch

———

The photographs were taken with
a 5 by 7 View Camera, lens Carl Zeiss,
Goerz-Dagor 1:6.8; F 30 cm.

———

Thou makest the beauty of form,
        through thyself alone.
Cities, towns and settlements,
    On highway or on river,
All eyes see thee before them,
    for thou art Aten of the day
        over the earth.

                        Akh-en-Aten

            Translated by James H. Breasted

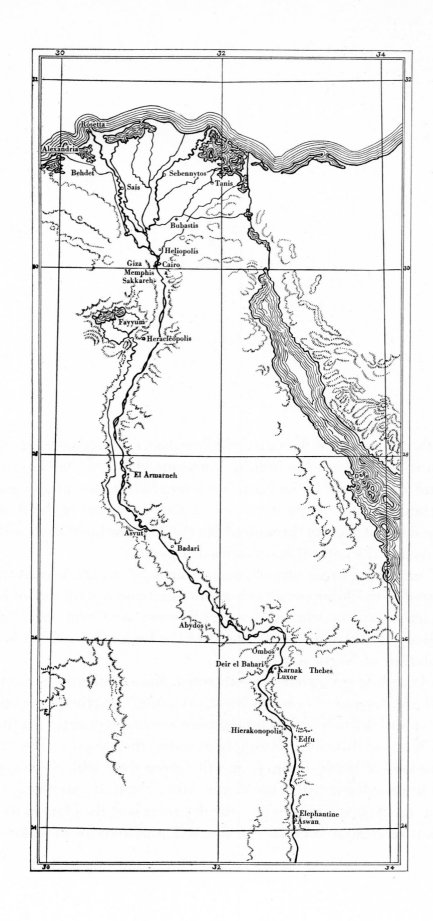

To the North, the stretch of flat coast with low dunes to break the waves of the blue Mediterranean; to the West, the infinite limestone plains of the Libyan Desert covered with sand and gravel; to the East, bleak and barren mountain ranges, cleft by canyons reaching out toward the coral reefs along the shores of the Red Sea; to the South, the rigid bar of granite through which the Nile has burst in a rush of crashing cataracts: these are the natural boundaries of Egypt.

"Egypt," according to an utterance once made by an oracle of Ammon, "is all the land watered by the Nile; and all those who dwell north of the city of Elephantine, the elephant isle, and who drink of that river's water are Egyptians." Egypt proper, thus, comprises only the northern expanse of the long valley which is cut into the vast desert plateau of North Africa.

Egypt and the Nile are intimately connected. More than mere accident prompted Homer to call country and river by the identical name: "Aigyptos." Egypt is the body of land through which the Nile flows as the main artery, feeding it with the very blood of life itself. Without this constant supply of water, the almost rainless region could never have become a fertile country, and the green oasis which is Egypt would lie dessicated, a lifeless desert valley under the African sun. By lavishing rich mud deposits upon it, the Nile was able to give the dry furrow of the plateau its good earth; and as a result of regular inundation, this soil produced an abundant life. In all

1

essentials, the development of Egyptian culture was determined by the Nile, or the "Haper" as called in Egyptian.

Every year, at the same time in mid-summer, the river rises from its banks. The need for controlling its course and for economically regulating the flow of its waters early taught the Egyptians the art of irrigation and the science of land surveying. In the starry skies they discovered the eternally immutable calendar according to which the rise and fall of each inundation could be calculated. Since the flood blotted out all borderlines, the agricultural sections had to be re-surveyed time and time again, and new entries accordingly made in the records. A feeling of responsibility was thereby evoked in the ruling classes, and with it the duty of making the common people property-conscious as well as inculcating an ever-increasing respect for the sanctity of ownership. As long as there was neither law nor strict authority to enforce the decisions of the judiciary, the annual inundation carried in its wake a constant renewal of fighting and conflict. Thus, the Nile became the creator of an orderly state.

When in the service of king and clergy Egypt's ingenious architects set about the task of erecting gigantic structures, the Nile served them well. It was the Nile which helped move the heaviest rocks and which carried the rafts laden with blocks of colored granite from the Aswan quarries in the South to the sites of the pyramids of Memphis and the temples of Bubastis, Tanis and Sebennytos in the Delta. The Nile, moreover, constituted the most convenient, often the sole road of travel and inspired the building of the artful rivercraft for rowing and sailing which we find represented in pictures of even the earliest periods.

The territory occupied by Egypt is comparatively small. Today its arable lands comprise about twelve thousand square miles, an area approximately no greater than that of Maryland. Nature has divided the country geographically into two equal parts which throughout history have preserved separate political interests: the narrow river valley of Upper Egypt and the broad lowlands of Lower Egypt.

The valley of the Nile has not always been inhabited by man. There was a time when the Egypt we know had not yet risen from the sea that reached as far as Upper Egypt, and the valley was still a huge lake. That the desert plateaus to the West and the mountains to the East, however, were already inhabited even at that time is attested by discoveries of flint implements which show little or no variation from those found elsewhere in North Africa or Western Europe. They belong to the last Palaeolithic Era, the so-called Capsian Culture, named after a city in southern Tunisia, the Capsa of the Romans, the Gafsa of recent military fame. We have no knowledge whatsoever of the people who developed this civilization. Neither a human bone nor a

2

single skull sheds light on the kind of man inhabiting Egypt during that distant period. But about eight thousand years ago, in approximately 6000 B.C., Egypt presented a distinctly different picture. By then, in all its geographical and geological aspects it was essentially the same country as the one we behold today.

The rains which had drenched the land so frequently during the previous millenniums subsided, and the formation of deserts to the East and West progressed rapidly. Consequently, the area comprising the present Libyan and Arabian Deserts became uninhabitable for any large mass of people. Its population began to migrate into the valley which, if not entirely hospitable, at least promised better pasturage and afforded ample grounds for fishing and hunting. The country abounded in swamps, and even the drier sections were dense with underbrush and trees. Choked in its sluggish course by heavy weeds, water lilies, and tall papyrus rushes, the Nile shifted constantly, leaving behind stagnant lakes and pools. In the marshes crocodiles and hippopotami threatened; in the low jungles and in the tamarisk and mimosa woods, elephants and giraffes, wild oxen and wild dogs were rampant. Human effort had to reclaim the wilderness for settlement and cultivation. The swamplands had to be drained, the jungles cleared, the beasts of prey slain or driven out. With unremitting energy, man had to subdue and conquer all the forces adverse to civilization.

The first settlers to whom fell the task of cultivating the soil were African tribes, members of an Afro-Mediterranean race, commonly called "Hamites." They were followed by tribes of the same race migrating northward from the upper Nile. After them came an influx of Asiatic nomad peoples who either were actually Semites or were closely related to the Semitic race at least in language: Assyrians, Hebrews, Arameans, Arabs. They all entered Egypt via the isthmus of Suez or the Red Sea. One human stream joined the next; different tribes intermingled. Gradually, out of this mixture, there originated a new people unified by a common tongue, the Egyptian.

This language, however, is known only by what is written on monuments of the historical era. Although the oldest of them was not erected before the end of the fourth millennium B.C., the texts are of a much earlier date. On this basis, the original Egyptian language must be classified as an Afro-Mediterranean tongue, next of kin to the Semitic and remotely related to the so-called "Hamitic" languages spoken by the East African peoples, the Bishareen, Galla, Somali, and the Berber in Northwestern Africa. The Egyptian vocabulary nevertheless contains certain additional elements of obscure origin which are most likely "African," as well as last vestiges of the vernaculars spoken by the aboriginal inhabitants of the country.

Therefore, Egyptian is a mixed language, predominantly Semitic but inter-

3

spersed with indefinable African elements. It was spoken in the land of the Nile from darkest antiquity to the Middle Ages, though naturally undergoing many transitional changes. A 1500 B.C. Egyptian would have encountered as much difficulty in making himself understood by his own countryman of the pyramid era in 2500 B.C. as would a modern Greek citizen in speaking to a Homeric warrior before Troy, or the Connecticut Yankee in attempting to join in conversation at the Round Table. Not until Egypt had finally been conquered by the Arabs (640 A.D.) was her language in its ultimate form—Coptic written in Greek letters—banished from its native soil and replaced by the speech of the new masters. Arabic, in a dialect all its own, is to this very day the language of Egypt.

For thousands of years Egypt and her people managed to survive the vicissitudes of history. The monuments preserved throughout the country bear witness to her ancient glory. From the heights of political power the empire was thrown into abysmal weakness. Grown rich by its own labor, the land was reduced to poverty by civil wars and laid waste by foreign invasions. Yet, after each new cataclysm, its people recovered and regained their vitality. Just as the soil on which they lived had its renascence every year after the flood, so were they reborn from recurrent disaster until death finally came to a body-politic sapped by ruthless conquerors.

It is a great joy, indeed, to behold the ancient Egyptian as he stands face to face with us in the works of his artists; to see him rough and rustic, or elegant and disciplined; to read from his features the gravity or gayety of the day in which he lived. But it is just as pleasant to meet him in his works of literature, or to learn his character and traits from his records and documents.

The Egyptians were of peasant stock, thoroughly noble and conservative, industrious and efficient. Misguided by superficial impressions, foreigners have either overstated their good qualities or underrated them with great injustice. Herodotos, puzzled by Egyptian customs and habits which were so different from those of his native Greece, praises their fear of God, their cleverness and uncanny memory. Diodoros pronounces them the most grateful nation on earth. But Hadrian, the Roman Emperor who visited the valley of the Nile in 130 A.D., decries them as "disgustingly light-headed, fickle, rumor-mongers," and calls them a "rebellious, good-for-nothing, vituperative people." The most prominent characteristic of the Egyptian, his conservatism, remained strangely unrecognized by all his critics. Nevertheless, this is his one trait that stands out everywhere, be it in religion, art or literature, writing or administration. With a faithfulness that borders on stubborn tenacity, he clings to whatever he has inherited from his fathers. He never forgets, never gives up what he

4

holds dear. With all the new he learns and acquires by experience, he keeps his traditions; he carries them, a dead weight, through the centuries like a cumbrous chain by the same token. Of course, the Egyptian people made tremendous progress in the thousands of years of cultural development, but slavish reverence for the past prevented every generation from full exploitation of its own opportunities. The vernal blossoms of Egyptian art, the budding thoughts of such reformers as Amenhotpe IV who strove for a certain monotheism, were nipped by the frost of traditional thinking. The Egyptian was deeply devoted to his country, his home and family. No greater misfortune could befall him than to die on foreign soil and be buried far from kith and kin in the desert lands of the barbarians.

There is justification, however, for reproaching the ancient Egyptian for a certain drabness and lack of imagination. A countryside with single-hued fields and monotonous palm groves does not give wing to fancy. In the lifeless tracts of sand, the desolate mountains and desert valleys, he was apt to see only a domain of death haunted by ghosts and evil spirits. Thus, Egypt did not produce a single great poet. No Homer nor Horace has ever sung his epics or played his lyre on the banks of the Nile. The hymns of the gods and odes in praise of the pharaohs are, of course, not entirely devoid of poetic aura. They contain many fine thoughts tenderly and picturesquely expressed, but their beauty is lost in an overgrowth of boringly repetitious phrases.

Despite her drabness and dryness, Egypt yet produced an art that outlived her political life by scores of centuries, masterpieces of which impress the modern world as deeply as they did the contemporaries of their creators. What commands our admiration may not be primarily the originality of conception and the imaginative genius of the artist. We are enthralled by his keen sense of observation, his intellectual soberness which, aided by a sublime craftsmanship, engendered the very best in human portraiture and in representation of animal life.

Egyptian art pictures the Egyptian people. The upper classes are well-bred, deeply cultured, and of a gentility which the common people try to emulate. Men and women alike wear only plain white garments, occasionally enhanced by patches of colored material and ample pleats. Gaudy colors and patterns are happily left to the barbarians. At home they surround themselves with comfortable coziness, endeavoring to give even the simplest furnishings a pleasing form and an adornment befitting their purpose—a principle which makes the Egyptian minor arts worthy of imitation to this very day.

The Egyptian gentleman was imbued with aristocratic pride but always inclined to be mild and just to his inferiors, preferring not to take advantage of his superior

5

social position. Cruelty was foreign to him, and dispassionate self-control his most cherished ideal. In earlier days, conquered enemies were killed; in later years they were condemned to do slave labor in quarries and mines; occasionally, rebels and traitors were decapitated and their heads publicly displayed as a deterrent. But these facts are by no means indicative of an innate spirit of brutality in the Egyptian or, for that matter, in any nation of antiquity. The Egyptian, however, would have abhorred sculptural reliefs showing his foe with nose and ears being cut off or eyes being gouged—as was the practice and pleasure of the Assyrians who gloated over such representation. The Egyptian always remained a gentleman who liked to look at the peculiarities of foreign peoples with a refreshing sense of humor and good-natured irony.

The people of Egypt were devoted to their gods. Firm believers in their divine power, they stood in pious awe before them and prayed for their grace and guidance. Akh-en-Aten, the heretic king who had torn down their altars and defaced their images, was considered by clergy and laity alike as the great sinner "who was felled" because he had dared touch Amūn, the king of gods.

No matter how religious the Egyptians may have been, however, it would be utterly wrong to fancy them as a race of puritans who lived with eyes directed toward the heavens, anxious to please their gods in order to be rewarded with a happier life in the Great Beyond. Certainly they devoted their most diligent efforts to the building of their final resting-places, and without regard for cost made endowments to secure for themselves adequate sacrificial offerings after death. This solemn concern nevertheless did not make them lose their faculty for making merry, although they never indulged in ribald revelry. Love, not lust; song and dance; beer and wine— these they considered the spice of life. There is an old banquet song, an invitation to joy, which had been recited in many versions to the accompaniment of the harp throughout the centuries ever since it was first sung about 2000 B.C.:

> ". . . The generations pass away
> And are replaced by new ones,
> Ever since the creation of the world.
> The kings who lived in times bygone
> Rest in their burial pyramids.
> The noble and the glorious departed, too,
> All lie entombed.
> Those who builded themselves homes,
> Their places are no more.
> Behold what has become of them.
> I have heard the words

Of Imhotep and Har-dedef (wise men)
Whose sayings are the talk of everybody.
How are their places?
The walls are rubble and destroyed,
They are no more,
Just as if they had never been at all . . .
. . . Nobody ever returns from thence
To tell us how they fare;
To tell us of their fortunes;
To give our hearts contentment
Until we, too, depart
Whither they have gone . . .
. . . Encourage your heart to forget
That you, too, will be a glorious departed . . .
. . . The sun rises in the mornings
And sets in the evenings.
Men beget, and women conceive.
Every nose breathes breath.
But when (another) day approaches
They already lie in their tombs . . .
. . . Follow your desire while you live.
Put myrrh upon your head,
And adorn with flowers
The body of your love
Who is sitting beside you . . .
. . . Do good unto yourself.
Put on garments of fine linen,
And anoint yourself
With the truly wondrous gifts of the gods.
Enjoy ever more the good you have,
And do not let your heart grow weak.
Do not grieve your heart
Til the day of lament arrives . . .
Let song and music resound.
Throw off all gloom and think of joy.
Be merry while the day lasts.
No man can take his goods with him.
Nobody ever returns from thence. . ."

Prehistoric Period
Before 3200 B.C.

Predynastic Period
4000-3200 B.C.

I

TYPHONIA

OMBOS

During the dark period of infancy through which the Egyptian people seemingly had to pass for thousands of years, an event of the utmost importance took place: the advent or invention of agriculture. Whence it came; whoever made the first plow; from what country and over what roads the various kinds of grains were brought into the land of the Nile: all these are moot questions. Nor can it be told with any degree of definiteness whence the domestic animals—ox, goat, and donkey—were introduced. Only one fact seems certain: that there existed some connection with Mesopotamia, i.e., Babylonia, which closely resembled Egypt in geographical structure. It is most likely, therefore, that one of the immigrating Asiatic tribes conferred the great gift of its agricultural knowledge upon the new homeland.

With the introduction of agriculture, the entire life of the Egyptian people was rapidly remodeled. Up to this point, they had eked out a bare existence, forced to live from hand to mouth on game, fish, and wild fruits. Now, by tilling the soil for only a few months, they were able to provide themselves with food that would last for a full year. Moreover, they had sufficient leisure to develop their innate artistic endeavors. The making of stone vessels and pottery improved; the flax they raised was spun and woven into fabrics. Cattle and goats provided the family with meat and milk. Step by step, their culture advanced, and the nomad hunters turned into settled husbandmen.

Several prehistoric settlements of this type have been unearthed by excavations in various districts during the last few decades. They bear witness to the evolution of this new civilization. The two most important ones were found in Upper Egypt, on the western banks of the Nile, south of Asyut. They are called the "Tasian and Badarian" cultures after the places of their discovery, the villages of Tasa and Badari. A third one was found in the Fayyum, the oasis in the west of the Nile valley, and others at the western border of the Delta, near Merimde-Beni Salame and in the vicinity of Cairo, at Maadi and El Omari.

Judging from the materials used by this civilization, it was distinctly Neolithic. Only the Fayyum settlement was bare of any copper or noble metals characteristic of the later stone age. This, however, must be ascribed to the singular poverty of the place, which yielded only the simplest utensils: arrowheads, harpoons and awls of carved bone; arrowheads and axes of flint; and earthen vessels of the plainest design. The other cultures, in all their primitiveness, were rich by comparison. The Badari settlers already lived in huts; they slept on wooden bedsteads with plaited rope-work and rested their weary heads on linen or leather pillows filled with chaff. Their pottery is surprisingly well developed. There is no great variety in form, but each piece displays perfect workmanship, quality of material and finish. Placed on mats and covered with other mats, the dead were laid as if asleep, but facing the settlement, the home of the living, so that they could keep an eye on their relatives and friends. The Badari people were husbandmen and hunters as game was still abundant in the desert plateaus. They raised cattle and sheep and goats, and even planted emmer wheat (triticum dicoccum) on small patches of arable land. Their apparent use of the throw-stick in hunting birds testifies also to their skill and dexterity.

Neither the degree of relationship between the various prehistoric cultures nor their succession has as yet been definitely determined. In 1894, however, the British archaeologist Sir Flinders Petrie discovered the only important milestone on the prehistoric road of Egypt. He found the culture of Nagada which, though still primitive, stands out from the others. It embraced all of Upper Egypt and Nubia, and immediately preceded the distinct culture of the Egypt of history. Its center, and presumably its birthplace as well, was the region of Typhonia, the country of the Egyptian god Typhon and his capital, the city of Ombos which stood on the site of the present provincial town, Nagada. It lived during the eight centuries of the Predynastic Periods approximately from 4000 to 3200 B.C. In the beginning, the Nagada Culture was still the culture of a people of hunters in which weapons, elephants, and hippopotami played the most prominent part. The early Nagada graves are circular

11

or oval pits. The dead are buried in a crouched position, lying on one side. They were supplied with all the necessities of a simple life so that they would not lack anything upon resumption of their mortal existence. The pottery which, everywhere and at all times, constitutes the main equipment of the grave contains food and drink. It consists of highly developed ceramics, thoroughly different from those of later historical times. Particularly characteristic are jars with a red polished surface; bowls and dishes with a shiny black inside and rim around the top; and red polished vases with geometrical patterns painted in white, or sometimes with designs of plants, animals, and human figures. Fine stone vases held exquisite oils and ointments. The flint implements display great technical skill. Slate palettes were used for grinding green malachite, the paint applied to eyebrows and eyelids either for merely cosmetic or for purely hygienic purposes. Very artistically decorated combs, hairpins, bracelets, and other toilet articles were worn by men and women alike.

Gradually, the Nagada Culture advances. In its second stage, the late Predynastic Period, many changes have already become manifest. The graves are larger, rectangular, and frequently lined with brick walls. Sometimes they are even divided into several chambers in order to provide additional space for the increasing amount of accessories. The pottery is also of a new type: yellowish or buff color, painted in a dark reddish brown. Its designs mirror the external world with striking accuracy. There are pictures of human figures; of flamingos and of desert animals as they are hunted in desert landscapes with pyramidal hills and fan-shaped trees; of curious boats adorned with a multiple fringe of oars and tribal emblems. Peculiar to this period are ball-shaped or cylindrical jars with ear-like or wavy handles.

Copper, probably imported from the Sinai peninsula, gains increasing popularity. It is used even in the making of common implements, gradually displacing flint manufacture which had become so highly developed.

The course of the Nagada Culture runs the full gamut of transition from the stone age to the era of metal. Whether or not this Predynastic Egypt was already familiar with writing of some kind is a question which cannot be answered, since none of the many hundreds of graves has yet yielded any written inscription. Unfortunately, therefore, we have neither records nor religious texts to assist us in the analysis of the political conditions or the spiritual aspects of that particular period. Yet there is some light in the darkness. Thanks to the Egyptians' conservative spirit, a great wealth of relics has come down to us. From these the archaeologist, with the aid of his imagination, may read the story of aboriginal Egypt in very much the same manner

12

as the palaeontologist tells the development of life on earth by means of fossil remains from the most distant past.

While the Egyptian people was bound together by the same language and enjoyed a certain community of culture, it did not start out as a political unity. Originally, the country was divided into a number of small tribal units which partly survived in the counties or, to use the Greek expression, "nomes" of the historical era. It is from the ensigns of the boats painted on the jars of the late Predynastic Period that we know many of these nomes. Since their traditional combinations resemble those of the later Egyptian counties, their identity can be established; and by their identity we learn of history before history.

The trend toward stronger political combines must have developed rather early. The tribes or counties of Upper Egypt united themselves into a kingdom, as did those of Lower Egypt. The two respective capitals were Ombos in the Typhonia (Nagada), and Behdet in the Western Delta, the Damanhur of the present day. The previously local god of each of these two cities advanced, by virtue of their becoming capitals, to the importance of a National Deity. For the Southern Kingdom the honor fell to Seth-Typhon; for the Northern Kingdom, to the falcon-god Hor. It is safe to assume that all this took place during the period in which the early Nagada Culture evolved and flourished.

History is replete with references to the "two kingdoms" or the "Two Lands" as they were called, and Seth and Hor play a more prominent part in Egyptian mythology than do any other pair of gods. Great wars were fought between the two kingdoms and their royal chieftains. In the end, Lower Egypt conquered the valley of the Nile, and the King of the North became the supreme and sole ruler of the land. For the first time, a United Egypt was created. Heliopolis, the On of the Bible, situated in the vicinity of the present Cairo and near the borderline of the "Two Lands," was made the capital.

This union seems to have lasted for several centuries. Then it disintegrated; once more the two original countries faced each other as independent kingdoms. But each realm kept Hor as its own National Deity. Upper Egypt prayed to him in her capital, Nekhen, the "falcon city" Hierakonpolis on the western bank of the Nile not far from Edfu, famous for its beautiful Hor Temple. And Lower Egypt honored him in Buto—the city of the serpent goddess Uto—of which not a single stone is left. All this apparently happened during the period of the Late Nagada Culture.

Considering their age-old enmity, it is not at all surprising that the two hostile

13

brothers, the two kingdoms, could not live peacefully side by side. New wars began to rage, during which, to quote a text of later days, "the Upper Egyptian kings put fright into the hearts of the Lower Egyptian."

One of these Upper Egyptian kings, whom we call "Scorpion" from the symbol of his name, rallied his forces successfully against the North. Final victory, however, was not won by him but by another king who appears on contemporary monuments under the peculiar name of "Nar-mer," and who is in all probability identical with the first historical king of all Egypt, Menes. Ever since his conquest of the "Two Lands," the pharaohs have carried the dual title of "King of Upper and Lower Egypt" and worn the double crown: the white crown of the South and the red crown of the North.

With the creation of the new union in the years around 3200 B.C., Egypt steps upon the threshold of history. The home and residence of King Menes, the Upper-Egyptian town of Thinis, the present Girga, becomes the first distinct milestone at the border of the Predynastic and Dynastic eras.

Dark as prehistoric and predynastic Egypt may be and may continue to be forever, we have at least a faint idea of the phases of her oldest culture, of the people who created and carried it through the centuries, as well as of the political evolution of the country. We know the seed sown in the soil of the remotest past, from which a deeper, stronger and by far more valuable culture was destined to unfold to glorious flower. The ancient Egyptians had no knowledge of their own early past. All they learned from their priests was that, before mortal kings began their rule on earth, gods had reigned for ages and after them demi-gods whom they called "servants of Hor" and whom we assume to have been the royal masters of the ancient kingdoms under the patronage of Hor. Next in succession, so the priest said, came Menes who, as Herodotos agrees, was "the first man" to rule over the whole Egypt. The Greek historian adds that this king was the founder of Memphis, that he constructed dikes to drain the country, and that he regulated the course of the river Nile.

From Menes to the reign of the first Psamtik (663 B.C.), Herodotos counts 341 generations which, according to him, comprised no less than 11,340 years, an historically impossible and incredibly long span of time. During this entire era, he says, no god of human face appeared, and the shape of the earth and nature's products remained unchanged. Men followed men, and neither gods nor heroes intervened.

Of this great age, from which we are separated by some 5200 years, the Egyptian priests kept temple records. From one of these annals which were written on papyrus, they read to Herodotos the names of one hundred and thirty kings. Extant fragments

14

of such records also list the names of kings and all the great events during each year of their reigns, such as the erection of a new building or a royal feast, and by far the most outstanding incident: the inundation of the Nile. The annual high water mark is painstakingly entered because upon it depended the calculation of taxes to be levied on the landowners, and in turn the entire administration of the state.

Similar annals were available also to the priest Manetho who wrote a history of Egypt in three books for king Ptolemy Philadelphus about 280 B.C. Manetho arranged the Egyptian kings from Menes to Alexander the Great into thirty dynasties. In the main, they correspond with the various royal houses which succeeded one another in the rule of the country, or, as happened from time to time, which reigned simultaneously. Modern historians have maintained the division made by Manetho. Yet, for the sake of greater convenience, they frequently combine several dynasties under the name of a "period" or "Kingdom" (Old, Middle, New Kingdom). As it is scarcely possible to determine historically exact dates for any dynasty or king prior to the seventh century B.C., the year of an event can only be approximated; and when it comes to the earlier periods, there may even be an actual discrepancy of as much as a full century.

Early Dynastic Period

3200-2780 B.C.

I Dynasty 3200–2980
II Dynasty 2980–2780

Old Kingdom

Pyramid Age 2780-2280

III Dynasty 2780–2680
IV Dynasty 2680–2560
V Dynasty 2560–2420
VI Dynasty 2420–2280

II

MEMPHIS

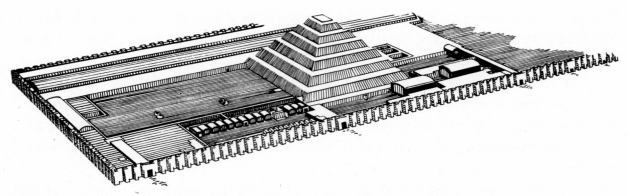

STEP PYRAMID OF SAKKAREH (RECONSTRUCTION)

Memphis is the gateway to the glory of ancient Egypt. From this great capital issues the story of the Old Kingdom which began with the Third Dynasty. Its landmarks are the pyramids. In six towering groups extending from North to South for twenty-five miles, they break the edge of the desert on the Nile's western banks.

Little is known of the kings of the First and the Second Dynasty, the immediate successors to Menes. Very few monuments are left of their time. Lower Egypt still seethed with insurrections which had to be calmed by brute force. Along the southern and western frontiers, wars continued to be fought against Nubians and Libyans, and especially against the "People of the East," the Bedouins of the Sinai peninsula whose valuable copper mines the Egyptians had earlier exploited.

The kings still resided in Thinis and were buried at neighboring Abydos which in later years became the sacred city of Osiris, the god of the dead, the "lord of the Westerners." The superstructures of their tombs which were built of sun-dried bricks are today but heaps of rubble. Only the subterranean burial chambers are preserved. Around a central room in which the king himself was laid to his eternal sleep, there were rooms for accessories. They included everything to keep the dead ruler in royal splendor for the life beyond: from ivory couches to oil jars of alabaster. But there was more which the king should not be called upon to miss. Certain members of his family, the queen and women of his harem, attendants who had been with him in life, the men of his bodyguard, dwarfs who had served him at court, and even his favorite dogs had to accompany him in death. There seems to be little doubt that the royal retinue was expected to join their master loyally in after-life. A cruel custom it was, though the opportunity of remaining at the ruler's side for an everlasting future

18

was well worth being sacrificed for. The same custom prevailed in the early days of Babylonia and was still practiced in Nubia at a time when Egypt had long since forsaken such barbarism.

The first king of the Third Dynasty which ushered in the period of the Old Kingdom was Zoser, undoubtedly one of the most outstanding rulers of his era. His face which we know from the first real human portrait-sculpture ever produced in Egypt —his life-sized statue in a seated position—shows an almost barbarically powerful intellect.

King Zoser moved his residence and court from the South to Memphis, at that time already the seat of the country's administration. While his predecessors, the kings of the first two dynasties, had chosen Abydos for their last resting-place, new royal cemeteries were laid out in the vicinity of the young capital. Zoser erected for himself the magnificent tomb known as the step-pyramid of Sakkareh. This monument has particular importance for the history of art inasmuch as it represents the first large structure of solid stone built in Egypt. Its ingenious architect was Imhotep. His memory was cherished by the Egyptians until the end of their history; and with good reason, for Imhotep deserves lasting fame equal to that of the master-builders of Greece, Rome, and the Renaissance. He was also thought of as one of the wisest men of Egypt. In later times he was idolized as a saint. He was to the Egyptian what Asclepios was to the Greek, the god of medicine and the patron of physicians.

As proof of his great wisdom a traditional tale was told as late as in Ptolemaic times. When under the reign of King Zoser—so the story goes—the Nile failed to rise and flood the land for seven long years and brought Egypt to the brink of ruin, the king turned to Imhotep in despair. He wanted to know from him where the source of the river was and who the gods were that governed its course. And Imhotep gave him his answer. In this case, however, the ancient savant seems to have known more than even our great African explorers who during the past century risked life and health in the discovery of the Nile's source. Imhotep told his king that the Nile sprang from the region of Elephantine at the southern borders of his kingdom (now the district of Aswan), where the river lay sleeping amid the waters guarded by the god Khnum. When the King heard that, he despatched a wealth of offerings to the goat-faced Khnum and the goddesses of the Elephant Isle. During the same night, Khnum appeared in the king's dream and promised him that the Nile would rise and flood the country again. And so it happened. Whereupon the king, in gratitude, presented Khnum with all the lands around the cataract of Elephantine which were to be held by him and his priests in perpetual and incontestable ownership.

19

The founder of the Fourth Dynasty was King Snefru, whose accession to the throne resulted from his marriage to Princess Hetep-heres of the old royal house. He conducted a glorious campaign against Nubia which supposedly yielded a booty of seven thousand captives and twenty thousand head of cattle, and succeeded in putting down a Bedouin rebellion on the Sinai peninsula. His victory in that region was so complete that he was praised for many centuries to come as its liberator and patron. His sepulchral monument is the Pyramid of Dahshur in the southern district of Memphis, where later his widow Hetep-heres was laid to rest by her illustrious son, King Khufu.

The peace of her grave, however, was soon to be disturbed. A gang of thieves broke into it and destroyed her mummy. Since they had evidently been disturbed in the midst of their crime, the other treasures remained untouched. The king was informed of the theft but held to the belief that the queen's body was intact. If he had known that the alabaster sarcophagus was empty, he would probably not have issued orders to replace its demolished cover and to take the earthly remains of his mother, together with all the sepulchral equipment, secretly to the royal cemetery of Giza. There she was, just as secretly, buried again in a well-hidden pit to the East of her son's pyramid. This second grave of hers remained concealed and unmolested for thousands of years until it was discovered by the Harvard-Boston expedition in the spring of 1925. Careful examination revealed among the many treasures of the subterranean chamber: the queen's household furniture, the gold-encased canopy and her bed with the head-rest, her armchair, a jewel box containing her anklets, razors, knives, and an array of other personal belongings. Every piece bespeaks the accomplished skill and the distinguished taste of the craftsmen of the Pyramid era, rarely equaled, and still more rarely surpassed by coming generations.

The Fourth Dynasty, which ruled for approximately one hundred and twenty years (2680-2560 B.C.), represents the culmination of the Old Kingdom. It was a brilliant, peaceful age of which the monumental tombs of its kings, the great pyramids of Khufu, Khaf-Rē and Men-kaw-Rē bear witness. All but two of the rulers of this dynasty were buried at Giza. Zedf-Rē, Khufu's immediate successor, evidently a recluse on the throne he occupied for only eight years, had his pyramid built in the solitude of the desert plateau near Abu-Roash, north of Giza, which is today a dilapidated, almost unknown monument. Shepses-kaf, the last king of his dynasty, also chose for his burial site a place far from the pyramids of his predecessors, in the southern district of the necropolis of Sakkareh. Departing also from the ideas of his ancestors, he did not give his tomb the traditional form of a pyramid but the shape

20

of a huge, barrel-vaulted sarcophagus which is known today as the Mastabat Fara'un, the "Grave of Pharaoh."

The dynasty of Snefru was dethroned by a family who claimed divine descent. It is related that the usurpers, Weser-kaf, Sahu-Rē, and Nefer-ir-ka-Rē, were triplets begotten by the sun-god Rē with the wife of a priest in a small town of Lower Egypt. Even at their birth, miraculous signs are said to have been given by the gods which predicted their royal destiny.

There exists an old Egyptian story which reads as follows: "Once, when their mother had a quarrel with a girl-servant and beat her, the girl turned to the other people in the house and said: 'She ought not behave like that, for she is the mother of three kings. Now, I shall go and reveal it to the king.' On her way to betray the woman to King Khufu, she met with her older brother in the fields, and repeated what she had said before. This made the brother angry, and he struck her. As she was about to scoop up a handful of water, a crocodile appeared and seized her. The brother went to tell her mistress what happened. He found her sitting in great sadness. When he asked her what her trouble was, she replied that it was brought about by the girl whom she had raised in her house and who had gone to denounce her to the king. The boy consoled her and told the story how the crocodile had seized his sister. . ."

Unfortunately, the story ends at the point where it promises to become most interesting. But its completion leaves little to the imagination. If the gods had not sent the crocodile to seize the girl, King Khufu would have learned about the triplets and undoubtedly done his best to destroy them. As it happened, the three boys were saved from his wrath so that they could grow to manhood, overthrow the evil king and his dynasty, and live as pious servants of their divine father, the sun-god, and all the other deities.

After they had become kings, they built great sanctuaries in honor of Rē. At Memphis, adjoining the present village of Abusir, these edifices were laid out according to the plan of the sun-temple of Heliopolis.

On a solid foundation, in an open court, stood the cult symbol of Rē, a mighty obelisk on whose gilded tip the sun reposed. In front of the obelisk was an altar of pure alabaster on which the pious offered their gifts and prayers to the god. Extremely beautiful reliefs, true masterpieces of Egyptian art, decorated the walls surrounding the court. Pictures of people, animals and plants at the various seasons, even an Egyptian landscape—the earliest known to us—are used to delineate a royal feast in all its glory.

21

STATE AND CULTURE

The united kingdom which Menes founded and his successors perfected was an autocratically ruled, patriarchal state and absolute monarchy. The king was the "god," the "good god." Embodying the falcon-god Hor, the lord patron of Egypt, he *was* the state and accordingly responsible for the country whose material wealth and power, whose very soil theoretically belonged to him. To the king all taxes were paid; every single one of his subjects was virtually his property through forced labor. The highest officials owed their positions to the king and nobody but the king. Princes and princesses of the royal house—and they used to be innumerable—were born incumbents of the most important offices. Above all of them stood the vizier as the immediate and most influential representative of the monarch.

It is characteristic of the prevailing patriarchal system that during the Fourth Dynasty this office was given exclusively to princes of the royal house, preferably to the crown prince. When the absolute power of the king began to decline during the Fifth Dynasty, this preëminent office passed into the hands of one particular family, with which it remained hereditary for generations. By the very end of this dynasty, however, the king chose to bestow it upon whomever he favored most among the great of his court.

For the career of the various officials, we have some information from their biographies. Numerous titles render proof of a well-ordered administrative organization, but the actual duties connected with each title can be established only in rare instances. Special training for civil service was not required. All that counted, and all that was needed for success in office, was certain practical experience and *savoir vivre*.

▲　▲

Economically, ancient Egypt was an agricultural state. Farming and cattle-raising produced its wealth. In this respect the Pyramid Age differed but little from modern times. But the widespread belief, already harbored by Herodotos, to the effect that the Egyptian peasant reaped his harvest with much less toil than other peoples is unfounded. Of course, the Nile renewed the earth by the annual alluvium of mud, and thus saved him the labor of fertilization. But otherwise he had to till the land in the sweat of his brow. He had to break the earth, hardened firm after inundation under the burning African sun, with his hoe—and a wooden hoe it was. The man behind the plow had to drudge as he did anywhere else. Seed had to be sown in

22

the ground. Sheep or donkeys were driven over and over across the field to stamp it firmly with their small hoofs. At harvest time, he set about working with the sickle. Sheaves of corn had to be bound up and carried to the threshing floor where the grain was trampled out by donkeys or cattle. The crop was then measured and stowed into sacks, the number of which was scrupulously recorded by a scribe. And then the sacks had to be emptied into bins. The Egyptian peasant did not have an easy life at all. Yet, his was the advantage that he could always trust the weather and was free from fear of the elements. The yield of his land could be reasonably figured in advance, providing that "no worms would steal one-half of the crop, and no hippopotami would come and devour the other," or that he did not have to report "there were also mice in the field, the locusts descended upon it, the cattle have eaten it up, and the sparrows have robbed it."

The grain the Egyptian used to grow was chiefly barley from which he baked his bread and brewed his beer, the favorite beverage of the nation since days immemorial. Besides barley, he cultivated two kinds of wheat, samples of which were found in various tombs. The often repeated story, however, that the Egyptian "mummy wheat" has preserved its germinating capacity throughout many thousands of years is sheer myth.

The large property-holders as well as the small farmers raised cattle, sheep, goats, and donkeys. Pigs, though pork was not prohibited, were not much in favor. Exclusive of chickens which they did not raise, their poultry was varied, including not only pigeons, geese, and ducks but also cranes, which were considered an especially fine delicacy.

Suffering, as all farmers do, from the hard work of the years, the fellah or Egyptian landsman lived in the hope of leisure in the Nether World. "There must be in heaven the field of the blessed, an ideal land where there is no wailing and nothing of evil; where barley grows four cubits high, and spelt (emmer wheat) seven ells high; where, even better, one has to do no work in the field oneself, but can let others take care of it."

▲ ▲

The political and economic integration of the unified Egyptian state since Menes was accompanied by a national development of its spiritual forces. Beginning with the First Dynasty, Egyptian culture progressed in every direction and, gaining ever greater momentum, reached standards never before attained.

Of basic importance was the invention of writing. During the preceding eras, thoughts which could not be conveyed orally had been promulgated only through picturization, a most primitive and imperfect medium of communication because of its lack of necessary uniformity. The step which the Egyptians took was as short as it was decisive. They transformed picture-writing into phonetic writing by clever selection of certain pictures which had become more or less symbols of the objects they described. These symbols were then used for the denotation of words or parts of words (syllables or letters) which equaled or sounded like those originally understood from the respective pictures. An alphabet was thus gradually formulated. We do not know when or where this new art was developed, but we have reason to assume that the birthplace of this "hieroglyphic system," as it is called, was the sacerdotal school at Heliopolis. No matter by whom and under what auspices the system might have been originated, its conception bespeaks astonishing intelligence and genius.

Concomitantly with the attainment of writing, which soon became the common property of all learned people in Egypt, a national art sprang into being. For the first time the greatest gift of the Egyptians reveals itself—a talent by which they were destined to become artistically the most prolific and proficient nation of antiquity, second only to the Greeks.

As if by spontaneous generation, sculpture grows from dormant seed. Almost over-night it attains such imposing beauty and massive proportions that it remains unsurpassed for more than three thousand years. During the first two dynasties, from primitive beginnings already discernible in the Nagada Culture, Egyptian art develops a distinct style of its own: the classic "Egyptian Style." Its center was Memphis and the great sanctuary of Ptah, that patron god of sculptors, painters, and metal-workers whom the Greeks ranked equal to Hephaistos, the divine protector of their own artists and craftsmen.

In the Memphis of the Pyramid era, the sculptors of the Fourth and Fifth Dynasties created the works which now grace our museums as the most famous examples of Egyptian art: in the Museum of Cairo, the noble portrait-figures of Khaf-Rē, and of the princely pair, Ra-hotpe and Nofret; the wood statue of the so-called "Sheikh-el-beled" (chief of the village); and the two statues of high priest Ra-nūfer; in Hildesheim, Germany, the seated limestone statue of Hemiun, a contemporary of Khufu; in the Louvre, the squatting scribe; in Boston, the effective bust of the prince Ankh-haf, and the portrait-heads of relatives and courtiers of Khaf-Rē; and last but not least, the delicate wall reliefs in tomb-mastabas of Ti and Ptah-hotpe at Sakkareh.

The fact that provincial Egypt also made artistic strides is confirmed by a diorite group of the Fifth Dynasty now in the Metropolitan Museum of New York: a notable

24

representation of the seated King Sahu-Rē, accompanied by a figure personifying the province of Koptos in Upper Egypt.

The development of art is paralleled by attainments in science for which the Age of the Pyramids must also be considered an historical milestone. The world's oldest book on medicine undoubtedly originated during the Old Kingdom although the manuscript we possess was written many centuries later, in about 1600 B.C. This book is known as the Edwin Smith Papyrus, and has been loaned to the Brooklyn Museum by its present owner, the New York Historical Society. It was published by the late James H. Breasted, the most distinguished American Egyptologist.

The unknown author of the papyrus text, probably a court or military surgeon, discourses on forty-eight surgical cases. The material is arranged according to the separate parts of the human anatomy, beginning with the head and ending at the feet. Discussion of the individual cases is covered by seven chapters in accordance with a schematic plan. The title of each chapter introduces an ailment, the name of which is given after examination of the patient and statement of the symptoms. In conclusion a medical opinion is added which takes one of three forms. It is either a favorable diagnosis, "an illness which I shall cure"; a doubtful diagnosis, "an illness I shall fight"; or an unfavorable diagnosis, "an illness that cannot be cured."

While the usual medical treatises of that era offer nothing but a random compilation of cases, the author of the Smith Papyrus scrutinizes his professional experience methodically and presents his knowledge in an orderly fashion. Besides its value for the history of medicine, his book also has documentary significance as evidence of the scientific spirit and the interest in research which pervaded at least some of the outstanding thinkers of the Pyramid Age.

Our knowledge about the purely secular literature of the same period is very limited. All that has been preserved is a few examples of rather sententious poetry, instructions or didactic treatises composed by famous fathers who wanted to lay down for their sons the rules for a good life or maxims of good behavior. They belong to the same class of Wisdom Literature as the books of aphorisms in our Bible; the Proverbs of Solomon; the Word of the "Preacher," son of David; or the Wisdom of Jesus, son of Sirach, in the Apocrypha. The earliest completely preserved example of this type of writing is ascribed to the vizier Ptah-hotpe who lived under King Isesy of the Fifth Dynasty (2500 B.C.). Two maxims from this book may be quoted here in the translation by Battiscombe Gunn:

"If thou be a leader, as one directing the conduct of the multitude, endeavor always to be gracious. Great is truth, appointing a straight path; never has it been overthrown since the reign of Osiris. One that oversteppeth the laws shall be punished. Overstepping is by the covetous man; but degradations bear off his riches. Never has evil-doing brought its venture safe to port. For he saith: 'I will obtain by myself for myself,' and saith not: 'I will obtain because I am allowed.' But the limits of justice are steadfast; it is that which a man repeateth from his father."

The other proverb reads:

"If thou be among the guests of a man that is greater than thou, accept what he giveth thee, putting it to thy lips. If thou look at him that is before thee (thine host), pierce him not with many glances. It is abhorred of the soul to stare at him. Speak not until he addresseth thee; one knoweth not what may be evil in his opinion. Speak when he questioneth thee; so shall thy speech be good in his opinion.

"The noble who sitteth before food divideth it as his soul moveth him; he giveth unto him that he would favor—it is the custom of the evening meal. It is the soul that guideth his hand. It is the noble that bestoweth, not the underling that attaineth. Thus the eating of bread is under the providence of God; he is an ignorant man that disputeth it."

▲ ▲

Just as Egyptian culture on the whole had a long climb to its first great height at Memphis, the ideas which led to the building of the great pyramids progressed only slowly and by degrees. They did not spring from the imagination of a single creative mind but developed from seeds of the past.

The prototype of the pyramid was the simple superstructure erected over the burial-place in the desert soil into which the dead and all their funereal equipment were laid. It consisted of a rectangular mass of stones or bricks. On the side toward the Nile Valley were two flat niches or false doors facing a space enclosed by low walls where offerings were made. This kind of tomb represents the so-called "mastaba." The word "mastaba," which means "bench," is a modern archaeological term taken from the vernacular of the Arab workmen employed in the excavations. In reality these superstructures do look very much like the slightly slanted adobe benches in front of peasant houses in the villages of present-day Egypt.

The cemeteries of Giza and Sakkareh are replete with such bench graves since they served as tombs for the nobility. One especially large mastaba is the brick struc-

26

ture erected in the vicinity of Nagada which, though once regarded as the tomb of King Menes, more likely belonged to a queen or some other prominent member of the royal family. Its steeply sloping brick walls are embellished with niches simulating the façade of a palace.

Of the same type are probably the oldest royal tombs at Abydos and a number of large brick mastabas belonging to high officials of the First Dynasty which have been excavated in the northern necropolis of Sakkareh.

It was Imhotep, the masterbuilder of King Zoser, who conceived a new architectural idea when he was charged with the task of building a tomb for his royal master on the edge of the desert plateau at Sakkareh. Imhotep fully realized that even the most massive mastaba could do nothing more than hug the sandy terrain. Its simple construction closely resembled a huge mound and offered little architectural contrast to the rolling vastness of the desert. To offset this impression of insignificance, Imhotep's plan called for a structure consisting of six mastabas—each level successively smaller than the preceding—to be placed one on top of the other to a stately height of approximately two hundred feet in all above the ground. His project further included the erection of a mortuary temple for the cult of the king at the northern foot of the step-pyramid, and of several additional buildings as well. The entire sacred precinct, the temenos, was sequestered from the outside world by a wall forming an enclosure fourteen hundred and seventy feet long and seven hundred and eighty-five feet wide.

Hewn stone was the material in which Imhotep decided to build. This again constituted a radical departure from the architecture of previous periods in which only crude bricks had been used even for royal tombs.

The center of the sacred area is the pyramid, which measures 413 by 344 feet at its rectangular base. Each of the six steps recedes about six and one-half feet and differs in height, the lowest one being $37\frac{1}{2}$ feet high and the succeeding ones 36, $34\frac{1}{2}$, $32\frac{1}{2}$, $30\frac{1}{4}$, and 29 feet, respectively.

The entrance to the pyramid is on its north side, at the foot of the first step. A passageway descends through the super-structure to the main burial chamber, which is dug into the rocky ground and lined with granite blocks. There is a rather complex series of subsidiary passages and chambers, at least in part created during subsequent attempts at restoration or by treasure-hunters. Some of the original chambers had their walls decorated with small tiles of blue-green faïence in imitation of woven reed mats. One of them has three niches, false doors, displaying the figure of King Zoser in fine low-relief.

The placing of the entrance to the Nether World on the north side was probably dictated by the religious belief of the ancient Egyptians that the soul of the dead king would fly northward to the "stars that do not know of setting," the circumpolar stars.

The mortuary temple north of the pyramid has unfortunately been destroyed to such a degree that it is almost impossible to reconstruct its plan. Nor can the respective purposes of the innumerable rooms be determined. Only one small chamber is preserved, the so-called "serdab" where the portrait-statue of the seated King Zoser was found as it had originally been placed.

Opposite the northeastern corner of the pyramid are two large mastabas, probably the tombs of two princesses of the royal family. Each of these mastabas has an interior chapel and faces a square courtyard of about eighty feet. The northern wall of the courts is formed by the façade of the mastabas. It is decorated with four fluted columns of the engaged type and two panels in a ribbed design simulating wood or reed used for protective purposes. Small engaged columns, formed exactly like single papyrus stalks and flowers, ornament the sidewalls. The ceiling of the chapel also has a strictly representative pattern of palm trunks like those frequently used in roofing the adobe houses of Egyptian peasants.

South of the two mastabas there lies a large oblong court, flanked on two sides by small chapels and enclosed by fences reproduced in stone. Stairs ascending from the inside lead to an almost wholly destroyed upper story with arcades of delicate fluted columns. It was within the open court that the royal throne occupied its honored place on a dais.

In all likelihood, this unique court building represents the festal temple where the famous royal jubilee, the "Thirty Years' Festival," was held in the presence of the nobles of all the land who had gathered under the skies in celebration of the great occasion.

Facing the southeastern corner of this Jubilee Temple is the only undestroyed part of the main wall. Resplendent facing-blocks of white limestone cover its inner structure. Niches and slightly protruding turrets, in turn enhanced by shallow niches, are intended to give the impression of palace façades.

A portal of two protruding towers leads to the monumental gateway of the entire sacred precinct, an oblong festal hall. It consists of a center aisle, along the main axis, and two side aisles subdivided into small cubicles. Forty pairs of cross-walls, piers displaying three-quarter engaged columns, used to support the ceiling. Top and base of these columns are carved out in imitation of reed bundles; false doors on the east and west sides simulate wooden doors standing ajar. Adjacent to the west side is a smaller transverse hall with only four pairs of similar cross-walls. It is evident that the architect had not yet dared to construct free-standing columns or pillars. Nor was he ready to create more than a nucleus of what was to develop into a real Basilica twelve hundred years later in the building of the festal hall of Thut-mose III at Karnak. There is a small temple building to the north of this hall, of which there remains little more than three cross-walls with fluted columns.

The reasons which guided Imhotep in the arrangement of the many structures and courts within the holy precinct are as little known to us as the practical purpose these elements were designed to serve. It looks as if he himself lost sight of the latter. Much as he actually did accomplish, he still could not cope with the diverse architectural problems confronting him.

The technique of working in stone was as yet incompletely developed. Everywhere there is evidence of Imhotep's imitation of the familiar brick masonry, and most of the details betray his dependence upon the older means of construction. Reeds are copied in the tiles that cover the walls; wood is simulated in stones representing the fences of huts. And the ancient brick-technique dictates, in no lesser degree, the method in which the niches of the enclosing wall are fashioned.

Most interesting of all is Imhotep's attempt to create roof supports in anticipation of real columns and to pattern them after the natural design of plants, as he also did on the façades of the mastabas for the two princesses. This innovation constitutes the very beginning of the plant-columns which play such a prominent part throughout the architectural history of Egypt.

Despite his imposing idea of multiple construction and his great decorative inspiration, Imhotep failed to reach the goal of a new monumental architecture. The employment of various old technical skills combined with too much traditional thinking prevented fundamental unity of style. The monument of Sakkareh is the accomplishment of a singular genius who created and developed his own individual form of building to a surprisingly high degree of charm and perfection. But it was too personal an art, it seems, to have been taken up by others. There was nobody to surpass or even to imitate Imhotep along the lines he established. An entire century had to elapse before a definitely new architecture was born and saw maturity at Giza.

The gigantic supplants the delicate; pyramidal step-mastabas are a matter of the past. Based upon a square foundation, with sides that are perfectly even and plain, rise the Great Pyramids.

It must be noted in passing, however, that the first pyramid at Giza was really not the first of its kind. The father of King Khufu, Snefru, had already entertained the

31

idea of constructing his tomb at Meidum in perfectly pyramidal shape. For reasons unknown to us, this particular plan was not carried out, but another tomb for the same Snefru was actually built near Dahshur in the form of a true pyramid—the very first one on Egyptian soil. The name of its creator, worthy of being ranked with Imhotep as one of the greatest architectural inventors, is unfortunately not recorded in the annals of history.

Inseparably connected with the building of the Great Pyramids at Giza is an entirely new system of planning. No longer are there scattered and heterogeneous structures such as those which Imhotep united by a surrounding wall. Now only four essential units are constructed: the pyramid proper; a mortuary temple to the east of it; a monumental gateway in the valley; and a long, slowly ascending causeway to connect gateway and temple.

The architecture of Giza, furthermore, shows tremendous progress in all its technical aspects. The comparatively small stones previously used were replaced by immense blocks. As to the general principles of construction, Greek authors have given us interesting accounts. Herodotos, in the second book of his History, relates that King Khufu compelled each and every one of his subjects to work for him. Some had to drag stones from the quarries in the Mokattam (the Eastern) mountains to the Nile and thence to carry them across the river in boats. Others received them there and had to drag them to the Libyan heights at the edge of the Western Desert. Each gang of a hundred thousand men worked for three months at a time.

According to Sir Flinders Petrie, these three months covered the period of inundation during which agriculture was at a standstill and the services of as many as a hundred thousand men could easily be spared. The stonecutters and masons were probably forced to work all year around.

"For ten years," Herodotos continues, "the people drudged in building the road over which the stones had to be transported from the Nile to the Libyan mountains. The length of the road is five stadia (3051 feet), its width ten fathoms (60 feet) and its elevation, at the highest points, eight fathoms (48 feet), and it is all built of polished stones and carven with figures. (Herodotos speaks here of the causeway from the valley to the mortuary temple.) Ten years were thus consumed in making this roadway and the subterranean chambers which the king had chosen to make the burial-place for himself. The construction of the pyramid required 20 years. Each of the four sides measures 820 feet and the height is the same. The pyramid is covered with smooth stones, perfectly joined, none of which is less than 30 feet long. This pyramid was first built in the form of a flight of steps. After the workmen had com-

32

pleted the pyramid in this form, they raised the other stones (those needed for the facing) by means of machines. These were made of short beams and hoisted the stones from the ground to the first tier of steps. Then they were hoisted to the second tier by another machine, for there were as many machines as there were tiers of steps. Or maybe, there was but one machine that was easily movable and could itself be raised from one tier to the next, as was required for lifting the stones. The uppermost part of the pyramid was thus finished first (by smoothing); the parts adjoining were undertaken next, and the lowest part, next to the ground, was completed last. It was recorded on the pyramid, in Egyptian writing, how much was spent on radishes, onions, and roots of garlic for the distribution among the workmen, and—if I remember correctly what the interpreter who read the writings told me—the total cost amounted to sixteen hundred talents of silver (approximately two million dollars). If this was really the case, how much more must there have been spent on the iron with which they worked, and on the food and clothing of the workmen."

New discoveries and recent research have added considerably to our knowledge of the architectural technique and the detailed construction of the pyramids. After the site for the royal monument had been selected, the ground was staked off so that the four sides of the pyramid would face the four points of the compass. Then, a large brick ramp was constructed which led from the edge of the cultivated area, periodically covered by the inundation of the Nile, to the safe plateau of the desert. Similar brick ramps would be erected while the building of the pyramid was in progress, but were removed at its completion since their only purpose was to serve as a scaffolding.

The pyramid itself was first built upward as a central structure of massive steps. These were then filled out with masonry and faced off with white limestone and partly with blocks of red granite.

The stones for the inner structure were quarried from desert bedrock of the immediate vicinity, while the facing-blocks had to be transported on rafts from the great quarries of Tura located on the eastern banks of the Nile, south of the present city of Cairo. Much greater, though, was the distance which the huge granite rocks had to travel. They were cut in the quarries of Aswan in the far South, cut to size there, and then brought on rollers or sleds to the Nile for shipment downstream. Many of the boats carrying this cargo were built on the spot from acacia timber which Nubian chieftains had to deliver upon order of the pharaoh.

The manner in which the building of the pyramids was organized was far from primitive. Of course, much was accomplished by merely taking advantage of great masses of forced hand-labor. But there was no lack of machinery either. In fact, the

33

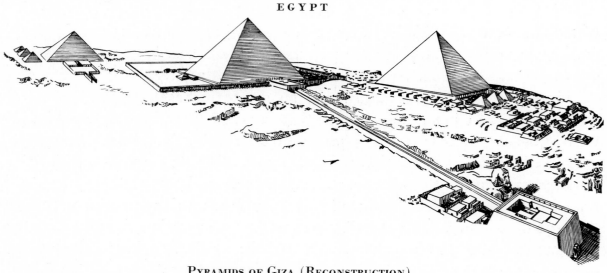

PYRAMIDS OF GIZA (RECONSTRUCTION)

Egyptians had rather well-developed equipment. The heavy limestone and granite blocks were lifted by various types of more or less simply constructed cranes. The huge pillars and colossal statues for the temples, for instance the mortuary temple of Khaf-Rē, were raised into position by means of scaffolds built of imported wood. Yet, despite all their mechanical resourcefulness, the amount of time absorbed in building a pyramid was enormous. Dates inscribed on blocks of the unfinished Snefru Pyramid at Meidum show that the work there extended over a period of seventeen years. Approximately two million cubic feet of stone were cut, transported, and utilized; in other words, more than a hundred thousand cubic feet annually, or almost three hundred cubic feet per day.

Based on these figures, the total completion of the Giza pyramids would have taken at least two hundred years. Inasmuch as their builders, the kings of the Fourth Dynasty, however, ruled only for a little over one hundred and twenty years, the efficiency of their building methods must have greatly surpassed that of Snefru.

In this connection, three rather relevant questions have repeatedly been asked in modern times: 1. How could a pharaoh like King Khufu for instance, when he ascended the throne and selected an area of 246,000 square feet for his monument, anticipate that his reign would endure for a period long enough to enable him to complete his plan? 2. If any one of the builders of the Great Pyramids had died during the second or third year of his reign, how could his son or successor, even granting his willingness, carry out the gigantic enterprise started by his father and

34

at the same time erect his own monument? 3. How would it be possible for many kings who lacked the boldness of a Khufu in predicting themselves a reign of twenty-five years ever dare begin a work of such dimension?

There is a rather simple answer to these questions—and a very convincing one at that. The pyramid-builders did not start out with a plan of extreme greatness. What they had in mind was usually a monument of moderate size, and in many instances their plan was carried out as originally conceived. Yet, it happened not infrequently that kings enjoying a long reign or finding themselves possessed with extended powers expanded the original design. They would enlarge their monuments either by mere additions without altering the passages or chambers, or by a revision of the whole original scheme on a greater scale. Occasionally, even a second enlargement was undertaken, as the Great Pyramid of King Khufu most prominently and best exemplifies.

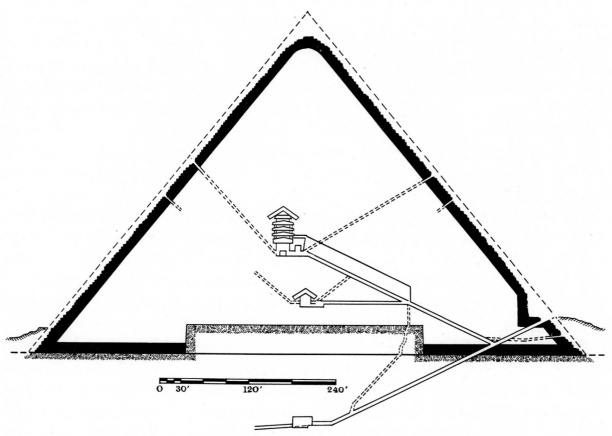

0   30'   120'   240'

CROSS SECTION OF THE PYRAMID OF KHUFU

35

The Pyramid of Khufu

Of the three Great Pyramids—the classic monuments erected by the Fourth Dynasty—it is the Pyramid of Khufu which captures the same degree of awe and admiration from the modern world as it was wont to command from ancient Greek and Roman travelers. The Egyptians called it "Akhet Khufu," meaning the "Horizon of Khufu," the place from which the dead king ascends heavenward like the morning sun over the Eastern mountains.

Today the shining blocks that once surfaced its gigantic triangles have disappeared except for a few on the north side. The length of its square base has diminished to 746 feet compared to the original 756 feet. Since its apex is gone, its perpendicular height is now 450 feet, while it is said originally to have measured 481 feet from the base of the inner rock foundation to the very tip. In like manner, the length of each sloping side has been reduced from 610 feet to 568 feet. The angle of inclination is 51°50′. The cubic content of the masonry, deducting the foundation of rock in the interior as well as the hollow chambers, used to be no less than 3,277,000 cubic yards, and still amounts to 3,057,000 cubic yards.

The interior of the pyramid, which has its entrance in the northern side at the third tier of stones, consists of a series of passageways, corridors, halls, and rooms. The tomb-chamber proper, commonly called the "King's chamber," is placed approximately in the center of the massive structure. It is completely lined with granite and roofed with nine enormous slabs of this material, each 18½ feet in length. At

36

present it contains nothing but an empty and mutilated sarcophagus of granite which bears no trace of an inscription. Once long ago, however, this sarcophagus held the mummy of Khufu.

From the realization that only a single room was used as burial chamber for the king, there naturally arises the question as to the purpose of the labyrinthine interior. Does it hold any mysterious secrets which the modern mind is not able to unravel? The story of how the pyramids were actually built provides the answer. The Pyramid of Khufu presents nothing special in this respect. The majority of the rooms originated from successive plans, and only a Great Hall, an antechamber, and the "King's chamber" were of the original design.

The Khufu Pyramid has withstood the ages. His mortuary temple is completely destroyed; the monumental gateway, the valley temple, is buried under the peasant houses of a modern village; and only part of the covered causeway is still preserved.

On the eastern side of the Great Pyramid lie three more pyramids, the Small Pyramids, built for wives of the pharaoh. Herodotos, however, insists that the one in the center was the tomb of a daughter of Khufu, of whom he relates in this connection: "So evil a man was the king that for lack of money he made his own daughter sit in a chamber and exact payment. She, doing her father's bidding, was minded to leave some memorial of her own and demanded of everyone who sought intercourse with her that he should give one stone to set in her work; and of these stones was built the pyramid."

This unfriendly story which characterizes the pharaoh as a wicked family tyrant, and which Herodotos was probably told by a gossiping "dragoman" is contradicted by the historical fact that King Khufu provided his favorite children with eight stately mastabas to the east of his own pyramid. And a second, grandiosely arranged cemetery for members of the royal house and faithful nobles adds proof to his generosity and concern for all those whom he wanted to keep as dear and near to himself in death as they had been in life.

THE PYRAMIDS OF KHAF-RĒ AND MEN-KAW-RĒ

The Second Pyramid which the Egyptians called "Wer-Khaf-Rē," "Great is Khaf-Rē," was erected by King Khaf-Rē, the son of Khufu. Owing to the greater elevation of the rocky plateau on which it stands, it appears to be higher than its actually taller neighbor. Its perpendicular height, originally 471 feet, is now 447½ feet. The length of its square base measures 690½ feet as compared to the original

707¾ feet, and the height of the sloping sides, inclined at an angle of 52°20', is 563½ feet in comparison to the original 572½ feet.

The casing, a substantial part of which is preserved at the top, consisted of limestone slabs in the upper courses and of partially unpolished granite in the lower ones.

The plan for this pyramid was apparently also altered in process of construction. The original intention of Khaf-Rē was undoubtedly to erect a small pyramid over a subterranean chamber. Later when he decided upon its enlargement, the chamber was moved southward to its present position. Consequently, there are two entrances and passages to the interior, both opening to the north side. One of the entrances was blocked up after the original building-plan had been discarded. The other, once 49 feet above ground level, leads to a descending passageway lined with granite in the beginning, continuing as a horizontal corridor, and ending at the burial chamber. This "King's chamber" is hewn into the bedrock and roofed with painted slabs of limestone.

The Italian explorer Belzoni, who opened the Khaf-Rē Pyramid in 1818, found therein a granite sarcophagus inserted into the rocky floor and filled with rubbish. He discovered no sign of an inscription.

East of the pyramid stood the Mortuary Temple. Although today it lies in ruins, the architectural arrangement of the entire building-complex is rather distinct. According to the requirements of the cult, it consisted of two main sections: one public and the other private. The same arrangement prevailed in subsequent mortuary temples as well as in the temples of the gods.

The most prominent part of the "Public Temple" was a large square court, surrounded in cloister fashion by an ambulatory and adorned with gigantic statues of the king. It was the place of assembly for the people and the court officials. To the sanctuary of the "Private Temple" only the priests and the chosen few were ever admitted. The place for the offerings was located in the sanctuary at the foot of the pyramid itself.

The imposing Valley Temple—or as it has long been called, the "Granite" or "Sphinx" Temple—formed the entrance to the sacred precinct. This ceremonial portico is a truly massive structure. Its rooms look as if they had been hewn out of the rock. There is no better example of the simple and majestic architecture of the Old Kingdom. Skill in working even the hardest stone material has herein reached its peak.

The main room is but a plain hall with walls of polished granite, in the shape of a reversed "T." Its flat roof is supported by sixteen rectangular pillars, of granite also, in front of which immense seated statues of the king were set.

Among all the monumental buildings of ancient Egypt none may be found in which sculpture served architecture more felicitously. The Valley Temple of Khaf-Rē, moreover, presented an unparalleled harmony of colors. The luminous white of the alabaster floor, the resplendent red of the granite walls and pillars, and the strange green of the stone statues blended together perfectly.

The Third Pyramid, named by the Egyptians "Neter-Men-kaw-Rē" or "Divine is Men-kaw-Rē," is the tomb of Men-kaw-Rē (the Mycerinus of Herodotos, the Mencheres of the Egyptian historian Manetho), who was the son of Khaf-Rē and the fifth king of the dynasty.

The present height of this pyramid is 204 feet (formerly 218 feet). The base measures 356½ feet and the sloping sides 263¾ feet, or, in line with the original facing-stones, 279¾ feet. The upper part of the casing consisted of limestone blocks, the lower of granite.

This pyramid, too, was built according to two or more successively designed plans. In its subterranean granite tomb chamber was found the richly decorated basalt sarcophagus of the king. This was unfortunately lost, for the boat which was bringing it to England sank off the Spanish coast.

On the east side of the Third Pyramid lies the mortuary temple of Men-kaw-Rē. Its ruins were excavated by the Harvard-Boston Expedition under the guidance of the late Dr. Reisner in 1907. The causeway, ascending from the valley temple to the pyramid, is still recognizable although the small brick temple itself has completely disappeared.

Thus the pyramids of Giza stand as eternal witnesses to the glory of ancient Egypt and the almost miraculous might of the pharaohs of the Fourth Dynasty.

Enterprises of such grandeur can only be undertaken in times of national prosperity; when state and government are firm and stable; and when no danger threatens from without. To think of the pyramids as monuments of tyrannical oppression and unscrupulous exploitation of a people by its autocratic rulers, as the "democratic" Greeks were wont to view them in the time of Herodotos, is intrinsically wrong. Nothing as great as the Great Pyramids was ever built on this earth without taxing a nation to its fullest capacity, without its straining every fibre in the accomplishment. Neither the Parthenon nor St. Peter's would ever have been completed without a certain brutality of rule and severe sacrifice of human life. Nor without force would a Suez or Panama Canal now be in existence. The ancient Egyptians did not take the

44

building of the pyramids as a particularly heavy burden or a monstrosity. All that the peasant subjects of the pharaohs knew was that they had to toil for their royal masters whether it was by forced labor in the fields, on the roads, or on other works of construction. The nobility also took great pride in the gigantic undertakings of their king, and likewise willingly dedicated their services to the pharaoh, descendant of a god and a god himself.

As the contemporaries of Khufu were awed by the divine efforts which had built the pyramids, so did the Egyptian world of future pharaonic eras raise reverent eyes to their supernatural height. To them they were creations of supreme energy and almighty power, giant relics of a giant past. Many a pyramid became the goal of pious pilgrimage. An Egyptian who thus journeyed to the Meidum Pyramid of King Snefru about 1500 B.C. wrote upon the wall of the mortuary temple—with the typical delight of the tourist—that he found the pyramid indeed "as high as the heavens," and then continued:

> "May heaven pour down upon this royal edifice a rain of myrrh and incense. Future visitors who wish for their children to inherit their offices should not fail to say a prayer so that the dead king may be offered many thousands of loaves of bread, beer, meat of beef and geese, sacrifices, meals, incense and ointments."

▲   ▲

THE "SECRET" OF THE PYRAMIDS

That the pyramids were burial-places of Egyptian kings was an undisputed fact familiar to the ancient historians. If Herodotos, in his extraordinarily clear description of his visit to Memphis, refers to King Khufu as the builder of the largest of the pyramids without also mentioning that the pharaoh was buried within it, he probably did so because this information would have been no news for the world of his day.

Diodorus states clearly that the pyramids were erected by the kings to serve as their tombs. The geographer Strabo, who wrote during the reign of Augustus, also speaks of the pyramids as royal tombs, adding that two of the three which he considered outstanding—those of Khufu and Khaf-Rē—must indeed be counted among the Seven Wonders of the World.

Arabian historians and geographers, to whom we are greatly indebted for their thorough reports on Egypt and Egyptian monuments, share the opinion of their Greek and Roman colleagues regarding the purpose of the pyramids. Never once did they question the fact that they were royal tombs.

45

There was no doubt in this respect until the early Middle Ages when Christian pilgrims passed through Egypt on their way to Palestine. It was evidently beyond them to understand why these monumental structures were built by so many thousands of workers just for the sole purpose of becoming the last resting-place for one single individual—even if he were the mightiest of all pharaohs. In their bewilderment, they began to look for what would seem to them a more reasonable explanation.

The Franconian historian, Gregory of Tours (540-594 A.D.), ventures the opinion that the pyramids were "elevators" erected for the pharaoh by Joseph during the seven years of bounty. Another medieval writer pretends to know that they were filled with grain even during the sixth century of our era. This legend is based upon a remark made by the Jewish author, Josephus, who claimed that the pyramids were built by the Israelites while they sojourned in Egypt. And there is indeed a grain of historical truth in his statement.

Many of the interpretations which made their appearance in modern times lack even the slightest degree of historical foundation. In this category belongs the fantastic notion that the pyramids had served as mighty levees against the waves of desert sand which otherwise would have deluged the fertile lands of Egypt; in other words, that the pyramids were a system of sand-breakers. Other writers expounded the theory that they were water works; and still others claim to this very day that the pyramids were not built by human hands at all but by the forces of Nature. Barely fifty years ago, a British author emphatically declared that the great pyramid of Khufu was a temple of Seth-Typhon, the devil of Egyptian mythology.

During the last century, an ever-increasing number of strange theories sprang up and rapidly spread all over the world. Their proponents have refused even at this late date to admit scientific explanations. Venturing into the twilight of mysticism, with numerological systems and mathematical calculations infallibly based on faulty measurements, self-styled "egyptologists" still try to read all kinds of secrets from the pyramids, and especially from the Khufu Pyramid.

One of the first and most zealous propagators of such numerological theories was an Englishman by the name of John Taylor, a book purveyor to the University of London who in 1859 published a voluminous work entitled: "The Great Pyramid, Why It Was Built and Who Built It." Two other volumes written by Piazzi Smyth, a fellow-countryman of Taylor's, were published in 1864 and 1867. Appearing under the titles of "Our Inheritance in the Great Pyramid" and "Life and Work at the Great Pyramid," they gained a reading public all over the Continent and even in America.

46

The main trouble with all of these books is that their authors work on the entirely false premise that as early as 2500 B.C. the Egyptians were already familiar with the exact relation of the circumference of a circle to its diameter. In other words, it is assumed that they had determined mathematical *pi* either in its accurate value of 3.14159, or at least approximately at 3.14286. However, an ancient mathematical papyrus admits of no doubt that even a full thousand years later the Egyptians did not yet have the slightest inkling of this ratio. The entire theory is thus based on a supposition of mathematical knowledge which the builders of the pyramids could not have possessed at that time.

Piazzi Smyth makes his deductions by dint of a measure he termed the "pyramid-inch." He determines the perimeter of the Khufu Pyramid as 36,542 pyramid-inches. Reckoning the day as equal to one hundred inches, according to Smyth this circumference would equal the length of one year. But he goes further. He multiplies by ten the height of the pyramid taken in inches, raises this figure to the ninth power, and thus arrives at the exact number of miles the sun is distant from the earth. Continuing still further in this vein, he takes the cubic content of the king's sarcophagus, including its cover, correlates this figure with the standard measure of the British quarter, and finds that it precisely equals four quarters, or four times eight bushels.

The great trouble with this figure, however, is again that it does not tally with official British publications which vary in their estimates of the old grain quarter.

As far back as 1885, the theories of Piazzi Smyth and his ilk were attacked by the astute archaeologist, Flinders Petrie. In his first great work, "Pyramids and Temples of Giza," he brands them as fantastic delusions. Under the magnifying glass of science, these nebulous speculations dissolve as completely as fog in the sun.

The architectural development of the Royal Tombs, from the brick buildings at Abydos to the step-pyramid of Sakkareh and from the pyramid of Snefru at Dahshur to the great pyramids of Giza, reveals the eternal "secret" of their existence. They symbolize the might, the magnificence, and the self-confidence of their builders, of whom King Khufu was the greatest. There is no other "secret" buried within his pyramid either. There was no supernatural knowledge about the cosmos, nor a mystical system of figures, laid to rest under its weighty stones. The glory of its builder—that was the message it was to proclaim to the generations to come. Its fundamental meaning may best be summarized by the words which a king of a later day had written upon the top stones of his pyramid: "Higher than the height of Orion is the soul of the king, and (in her depth) she unites herself with the Nether World."

47

THE SPHINX

In front of the three Great Pyramids and their mortuary temples lies a fourth equally famous monument: the Sphinx. The symbolic guardian of the sacred royal burial ground is a colossal recumbent lion crowned with the head of a king in royal head-dress bearing the uraeus serpent, the emblem of royal dignity.

The total height of the monument is about 66 feet; its over-all length 240 feet. The ear measures $4\frac{1}{2}$ feet, the nose 5 feet 7 inches, the mouth 7 feet 7 inches, and the extreme breadth of the face $13\frac{3}{4}$ feet. The head is now deplorably mutilated. The neck has become too thin; nose and beard are broken off; and the reddish tint which once enlivened the body has almost disappeared. Yet, despite disfigurement and attendant disproportion, the impression of strength and majesty is unimpaired.

The Sphinx lies in the center of a large quarry which once supplied King Khufu with stone for the building of his pyramid. In the course of quarrying operations, a knoll of hard grey and soft yellowish limestone was left untouched because it lacked the quality of good building material. When Khaf-Rē erected his own pyramid years later, this mass of rock attracted the attention of the king and his builders, and gave them the happy idea of shaping it into a lion with a human face in the image of the pharaoh. It is an old Egyptian literary concept that the king is a lion who strikes down his foe by means of his powerful paws.

The royal Egyptian Sphinx—it may be emphasized—has no connection whatsoever with the female sphinxes of Grecian mythology and art. The Greeks never called it by that name but used the Egyptian appellation, "Harmachis." It has been known as "Sphinx" only since the eighteenth century when classical archaeology chose to apply this misnomer most ineptly to a monument born of the purest Egyptian spirit.

However, the origin of the Sphinx, as well as the fact that it represented the image of a king, had already been forgotten in the New Kingdom. It was considered a personification of the sun-god, as implied by the name "Harmachis" meaning "Hor (the sun-god) on the Horizon." And as the image of Hor it enjoyed the reputation of special sanctity.

First evidence of this transformation is manifested at the beginning of the New Kingdom when Amen-mose, the eldest son of King Thut-mose I (1525 B.C.), in commemoration of a visit made a sacrificial gift to the small temple of Harmachis. Some scores of years later, another illustrious visitor, the crown prince Amen-hotpe II (1450-1420 B.C.), visited Harmachis. As a youth he was a great sportsman, an

48

excellent archer, and a lover of horses. The inscription on a memorial stone, found several years ago, describes him as follows:

"He trained steeds that had no equal. They never tired when he held the reins, nor did they get into a sweat at a gallop."

One day when it pleased him to make an excursion all by himself, "he harnessed his horses in all secrecy, and stopped at the sanctuary of Harmachis. There he spent a little while, pacing hither and thither, examining the fine arrangement of this sanctuary of Khufu and Khaf-Rē. He wished to keep their names alive till the day when his father Rē endowed him with kingship. After His Majesty was crowned, and the uraeus, the symbol of Rē, was fastened on his forehead . . . the land was in peace as at the beginning (of time) under its master. He ruled over the 'Two Lands'; all foreign countries lay gathered under his sandals. Then, His Majesty remembered the spot where he once had relaxed in the neighborhood of the pyramids and of Harmachis. It was ordered that a sanctuary should be built there in which a stela of limestone was to be placed and inscribed with the King's name: 'Rē-is-great-of-Appearance,' loved by Harmachis, endowed with eternal life."

The Sphinx had a perpetual enemy in the sand of the desert which again and again buried his body. Repeatedly, he had to be freed; the first time probably upon the royal edict of Thut-mose IV, the son and successor of Amen-hotpe IV who had also inherited his father's love of sports. He himself tells us most vividly the reasons for saving the Sphinx from the sand in a memorial stela which he ordered placed between its fore-paws. Therein he says that "he, before his ascent to the throne, entertained himself as prince with desert hunts in the vicinity of Memphis. One of these excursions took him one day to Harmachis. It was noon-time. Tired, he sat down in the shade of the "great god." When the sun reached the zenith, he fell asleep and beheld the majesty of the august god, who spoke to him with his own mouth as a father to his son: 'Look upon me and behold me! Oh my son Thut-mose. I am thy father Harmachis, Khepri-Rē-Atum (names by which the sun-god was also called). I shall give unto you the kingdom upon earth, and you shall wear its red crown and its white crown. . . For a great number of years my face has been turned toward you, and my heart likewise. You shall be to me the one to carry out my will, for I am suffering in all my perfect body. The sand of the desert, on which I stand, is pressing upon me. Hasten to me and do what is in my heart, for I know that you are my son and my patron, and I am with you."

When the prince awakened, he thought of the words of the god, and they remained in his memory. Thus, in the very first year of his reign, he fulfilled the request

50

of the god who had bestowed sovereignty upon him, and ordered the removal of the sands which by that time had almost buried the Sphinx. Of course, his efforts had but a temporary effect. From time to time, and as recently as 1926-1927, the Sphinx has had to be freed again from the eternally rolling sand of the desert.

Today the "great god" looks upon us as majestically as he greeted King Khaf-Rē, whose royal image he was, so many thousands of years ago. In monumental character, the Sphinx equals the pyramids. As a work of art it renders proof that Egypt in those early days had mastered monumental sculpture in no less degree than architecture.

▲ ▲

The Later Pyramids, and the Pyramid Texts

The Fourth Dynasty definitely established the basic type of the Royal Tomb. In its architectural details it was naturally subject to change. The funeral monuments of the Fifth Dynasty at Abusir, for instance, express a more modern style and exhibit a greater richness. The ponderous massiveness which characterized the Great Pyramids gives way to a more pleasing lightness. Bare, square stone pillars are replaced by columns reflecting forms of the Egyptian flora: papyrus, lotus, and palm. The walls of the mortuary temple are no longer plain, but adorned with colored reliefs in order to impress the people with the greatness of their royal ruler. Multi-figured pictures tell of the king's victories by showing how bound captives, each representing another conquered people, and the rich booty taken in the enemy's country are brought before the pharaoh.

At the end of the Fifth Dynasty, the pyramid builders introduced another innovation. With the exception of the step-pyramid, the burial chambers had neither pictures nor inscriptions. Then King Unis covered their walls with extensive hieroglyphic texts, the so-called "Pyramid Texts." Their contents were not new, but had been known from time immemorial. Like the Indian Vedas or the Homeric epics, they had been passed on by word of mouth from generation to generation until they were finally written down on papyrus, probably during the early dynastic era. From these writings, they were recited at funeral celebrations by the priests. Now, in order to assure himself of their benefit for all eternity, the king had them copied on the walls of his tomb so that he could read them without priestly assistance, which might after all fail him some day.

The main purpose of these texts is to tell that the illustrious deceased is not going

51

to live like a common mortal in the dark regions of the Nether World, but in the heavens and in the company of the sun-god in whose stead he may even rule over the world. By virtue of their magic power, the recitations are supposed to help the king on his road to heaven. They advise him how to reach it. He may either climb up to it on stairs which are built for him, or fly to it as a goose or a beetle and seat himself upon the throne in the boat of the sun-god.

"He flies away from you, mortals; he is no longer upon earth but upon the heavens. He has darted to heaven as a heron; he has leaped to heaven as a locust."

Those who dwell in the celestial domain are frightened when the deceased pharaoh reaches the skies. Even the sun-god himself is seized with terror when a messenger tells him that an "indestructible spirit" has arrived—his son, with whom he will wander through the heavens. For the dead king has power over life and death. "Whom he wants to live, shall live; but whom he wants to die, shall die."

The entire universe is thrown into an uproar. "The skies pour out water; the stars darken; the bones of the earth tremble; the cosmos ceases to move when they see him appear endowed with life. He is the Lord of Wisdom—whose mother knows not his name. His glory is in the skies; his power is in the horizon like Atum (the sun-god of Heliopolis), the father who begat him; as he begat the king, the king was mightier than he."

But he is also a god of horror "who lives on his fathers and feeds on his mothers. . . . He devours men and lives on gods." The gods themselves assist him in preparing his cannibalistic meals. "One god catches them with a rope, another watches over them and drives them before him. . . The God of the wine-press carves them up and cooks parts of them in his evening cooking vessels . . . the tall ones are his ration for the morning; the medium-sized for the evening; and the small ones for the meal of the night. The old men and old women (unfit to eat!) are for his incense-burning." The inner organs—heart, lung, and viscera—are all eaten while the legs of the victims are used for fuel or for wiping the cooking pots clean.

The purpose of this cannibalism is unmistakably clear. By devouring the bodies of the gods, the pharaoh obtains not only physical nourishment but becomes possessed of their divine powers and qualities. "He has swallowed the intelligence of every god . . . their magic is in his belly; . . . he eats their magic and swallows their spirit."

By this absorption of the combined power, intelligence, and magic of the gods, the pharaoh comprises in his own person all the attributes of divinity, and himself becomes the supreme and omnipotent deity. One of the texts says so in the plainest

52

of terms: "A warrant of appointment as 'Great Mighty One' is given to him by Orion, father of the gods . . . he has power over the mighty ones . . . he endows with divinity the great figures of the gods." His life becomes everlasting, he is free to act as he desires, and if he so wishes he can mingle with those who are still living on earth.

Distinctly different in their ideology are many texts marked by features of the pre-historic Osiris myth. James H. Breasted, in his "Dawn of Conscience" (1933), has formulated these ideas in his own inimitable way: "The complete identity of the dead king with Osiris, 'lord of the Nether World,' is set forth. The king becomes Osiris and rises from the dead as Osiris had done. This identity began at birth and is described in the texts with all the wonders of a divine birth. Osiris himself under various names is adjured: 'Thy body is the body of this king; thy flesh is the flesh of this king; thy bones are the bones of this king. As he (Osiris) lives, this king lives; as he dies not, this king dies not; as he perishes not, this king perishes not.' Thus the dead king receives the throne of Osiris, and becomes like him, king of the dead. 'How beautiful is this!—How beautiful is this which thy father Osiris had done for thee (the King)!—He has given thee his throne, thou rulest those of hidden places (the dead), thou leadest their august ones; all the glorious ones follow thee."

The supreme boon which the identity of the king with Osiris assured to the dead pharaoh consisted in the good offices of the son of Osiris, Hor, the personification of filial piety. All the pious attention which Osiris had once enjoyed at the hands of his son Hor now becomes the king's portion also.

These quotations from the Pyramid Texts, whose full meaning is difficult for the layman to understand, may show that they are not part of a homogeneous literary work. The Pyramid Texts do not represent a systematic compilation of the ideas concerning the life of the king after death. Nor do they record any data about the governmental activities of the pharaoh whose burial chamber they adorn. Yet they are invaluable documents for the student of Egyptian religion, as well as for the grammarian because of their ancient phraseology.

The End of the Old Kingdom

The magic texts in the pyramids of Sakkareh promised to endow the kings of the Fifth Dynasty in heaven with such supernatural strength that even the gods would tremble at their sight. This, however, did not apparently correspond to their actual power on earth.

Unis, the last representative of this dynasty, lost his throne probably as the victim of a revolution. The kings of the new royal house succeeded in re-establishing some semblance of order, but the power of the Sixth Dynasty was unstable and steadily decreased. Particularly feeble was the reign of the aged Pepy II who ascended the throne as a six-year-old child and occupied it for ninety-four years. His extended reign, with the concomitant weakness of government, resulted in a disastrous revolution and the final collapse of the Old Kingdom.

The officials of the state, once the strongest supporters of the kingdom and its most intimate constituents, had gradually detached themselves from it and usurped an ever greater independence. They grew haughty and self-seeking. The administration at large began to disintegrate and carried the entire state to its doom.

Where the revolt started, who aroused the people against their oppressors, and whose hand guided the rebellion, is probably forever shrouded in impenetrable darkness. Unaware of the happenings without, the aged king Pepy II sat in his palace. He may have learned the bitter truth from one of his advisers. An old sage narrates in a papyrus that "the king saw the walls destroyed and could not raise an opposing finger. The offices of the officials were stormed, and the records were destroyed. Serfs became lords. The land was in revolution like a potter's wheel. Those high in council were starving, and fat citizens had to sit tending the mills, instead of the serfs. The children of the great were struck against the walls; the dancing girls were thrown into the desert. The highest honors fell upon women serfs around whose necks hung precious ornaments, while those who had been ladies went about in rags and a-begging through the country." A famine broke out. "Nourishment was taken from weeds, and water was drunk; and, for hunger, the fodder was taken away from swine. The cultured man had but the one and only wish: 'May the people perish, and may no more be born.'" The fury of the people did not spare the person of the king. His palace was attacked, and his residence collapsed. The rule of the mob commenced; "those who had been poor before, became suddenly rich; the up-starts are ruling, and the officials of the old Kingdom are now their courtiers."

The political misfortunes of the land had not yet reached a climax; even greater misery was still in store. The eastern boundaries of Egypt suffered warlike attacks by foreign forces, probably by Semitic peoples from Asia. The enemy entered the Delta, laid its cities in ashes, and ruled there for a while. The patriarchal Old Kingdom was dethroned. Gone was the glory of the Pyramid era, and Memphis, the proud capital of the "Two Lands," lost its lustre for centuries to come.

First Intermediate Period

2280-2060

VII–VIII Dynasty 2280–2240
IX–X Dynasty 2240–2060

Middle Kingdom

2060-1780

XI Dynasty 2060–2000
XII Dynasty 2000–1780
XIII Dynasty 1780

Second Intermediate Period

1780-1546

XIV–XV Dynasty 1780–1730
XVI–XVII Dynasty 1730–1546

III

FAYYUM

Sapped by the selfishness of its officials, the royal line of Memphis was dying of old age. The princes who ruled in the provinces, however, not only maintained their position and steered clear of the general chaos but even increased their power. Thus it was they who became the pioneers of reconstruction.

Some of the independent principalities which arose within the ancient provinces, the nomes, expanded beyond their original boundaries and developed, a few decades after the revolution, into a group of petty kingdoms. The sense of order, one of the strongest attributes of the Egyptians, finally triumphed over the utter confusion of the times.

One of these new kingdoms, the Heracleopolitan Kingdom, embraced the Delta and had its southern boundary in the district of Thinis, the capital of the first two dynasties. It was ruled by the princes of Heracleopolis, the modern Ehnasya in Middle Egypt, and endured for about two centuries from 2240 to 2060 B.C. (Ninth

58

and Tenth Dynasties). Its founder, Akhthoes, once more assumed the full titulatory of the ancient pharaohs, regarding himself as the incarnation of the royal patron-god Hor, "He who is loved by the Two Lands," i.e., Upper and Lower Egypt. This was rather presumptuous since a considerable portion of the Two Lands, the southern part from Thinis upstream to Aswan, hardly ever came under his rule.

According to Greek tradition, Akhthoes was "the most wicked of all pharaohs up to his time. He spread evil all over Egypt, was seized by insanity, and in the end was devoured by a crocodile." This obviously exaggerated story may even be completely false inasmuch as it seems to confuse two kings of the same name.

The end of Egypt's political partition and the restoration of her unity was brought about by Thebes in Upper Egypt, a territory which had played only a subordinate role in the Old Kingdom. Its princes, all of whom bore the name Intef, succeeded in extending the authority of their house beyond their own nome and in dominating Upper Egypt as far as the border of the Heracleopolitan Kingdom. They soon began to call themselves "Kings of Upper and Lower Egypt" despite the fact that they held the southland only.

After an initial period of peaceful relations with the northern state, wars broke out which ended in the victory of the South under the Theban Mentu-hotpe II (about 2065 B.C.), the founder of the Eleventh Dynasty. The Heracleopolitan Kingdom was completely destroyed, but it took three score years until the power and unity of Egypt were fully re-established. Peace gradually returned to the sorely tried country. The year 2065 B.C. marks the end of an interregnum, the so-called First Intermediate Period, and the beginning of the new era, the Middle Kingdom.

The first king of the Twelfth Dynasty, Amen-em-hēt, it is recorded, "traveled, shining like Atum (the sun-god), through the country in order to uproot injustice and to restore that which he found destroyed. He separated the districts one from another, and taught each city to know the boundaries shared with the next, and to establish its boundary-stones as firmly as the heavens. He judged their irrigation rights from what he found in the records, and determined their districts according to what was specified in the ancient writings because he loved truth (justice)."

With special care, the king looked after the welfare of his subjects. Rightfully he could boast: "I planted gardens and loved the harvest-god; the Nile greeted me in every valley. Nobody went hungry in my years, and none ever thirsted." Yet, in every quarter Amen-em-hēt does not seem to have found the gratitude and affection he expected. At least one serious conspiracy was planned against him. In the darkness of night he apparently was attacked by enemies and managed only with great diffi-

59

culty to escape the would-be assassins: "The halls of the palace rang with the clash of arms, and the life of the king was in danger."

In the twentieth year of his reign, Amen-em-hēt—for reasons beyond our grasp —made his own son co-regent. His name was Sen-Wosret ("The man of the Goddess Wosret"), Grecized Sesostris. This co-regency was the first of its kind in the history of Egypt though often imitated in later times.

In 1970 B.C., after a reign of thirty years, Amen-em-hēt died. "He disappeared into the heavens and was joined with the sun; the descendant of the god returned to his creator. The residence was benumbed; all hearts were filled with sorrow. The two great doors of the palace were closed. The courtiers, heads upon their knees, sobbed, and the people mourned."

When this portentous death occurred, Sen-Wosret, the heir to the throne, was far away from the capital on a campaign against the Libyans, the western neighbors of Egypt. His adherents despatched messengers to bring him the sad tidings. "They met him on the way; they reached him at nightfall. Never had he been in such haste; he, the falcon, flew with his followers; the army knew not of his departure."

The period of the Twelfth Dynasty was an era of economic prosperity and flourishing cultural life. Its peacefulness and inner political stability may be judged by the long undisturbed reigns of its kings. Son followed father with uninterrupted regularity. Sen-Wosret I occupied the throne for forty-five years, and each of his successors, who were traditionally named either Sen-Wosret or Amen-em-hēt, reigned almost as long.

The princes and kings of the Eleventh Dynasty had maintained Thebes as the capital. The tombs which they built for themselves on the western banks of the river reflect the modesty of their earthly power. These consisted of small brick pyramids with adjoining buildings laid out similarly to the royal tombs of the Old Kingdom. Mentu-hotpe was the first again to erect for himself and his successor a truly royal monument. Its ruins under the cliffs of Deir el Bahri still bespeak his mighty personage.

Amen-em-hēt I moved the capital to the center of the country, in the vicinity of Memphis where the seat of the government remained during the Twelfth Dynasty. It was a clear demonstration of the fact that the hub of the kingdom no longer lay in the South. As once before, under the kings of the Pyramid Age, it shifted to what the Egyptians termed the "Balance of the Two Lands," the boundary line of Upper and Lower Egypt. The king named his residence most characteristically "Conqueror of the Two Lands." The city was located twenty miles south of the Memphis of the Sixth

60

Dynasty, near the modern village of Lisht where Amen-em-hēt and his successor Sen-Wosret I also built their pyramids and mortuary temples amid the mastabas of the kingdom's great ones. They have reappeared from the desert sands as a result of careful excavations undertaken by the Metropolitan Museum of New York. At Dahshur, north of Lisht and still closer to the ancient Memphis, were the residences and tombs of Amen-em-hēt II and III as well as of Sen-Wosret III.

Sen-Wosret II had removed his court from the Nile Valley to the Fayyum oasis, near the present village of Lahun, and built his earthly and eternal residence there. The same district, neighboring on the village of Hawara, was also later chosen by Amen-em-hēt III for his palace and a second tomb. His once magnificent but now almost completely destroyed mortuary temple, the so-called Labyrinth, was greatly admired by Greek and Roman travelers. It is well described by Strabo; and Herodotos reports that it not only surpassed the pyramids in grandeur but was more imposing by far than any Greek building, the temples of Ephesus and Samos included.

The most glorious and enduring accomplishment of the Twelfth Dynasty, however, was the reclamation of the marsh land of the Fayyum. From the earliest days a branch of the Nile had irrigated this large desert oasis. During inundation, surplus waters used to overflow the natural basin and swamp the entire district so that its lower parts became a huge stagnant lake filled with crocodiles. Now, this area was drained and made fit for agriculture. Locks were constructed at the entrance to the oasis; canals were dug; arable land was protected by dikes against the dangers of the lake. Thus the "Lake-Land" became the most fertile and thriving province of Egypt —and has remained so ever since.

▲ ▲

In the beginning of the Middle Kingdom, the internal structure of Egypt presents an entirely new aspect. The bureaucratic state of the Pyramid Age, the absolute monarchy, has become a feudal kingdom. The independent princes ruling in the nomes conduct themselves almost as kings in their own right. When one of them comes to the capital, he is received at court with royal ceremony. "He went into the presence of his lord; the court officials followed him; the guards at the doors stood with bowed heads until he had come to the place where His Majesty was."

The spirit of self-reliance manifests itself most conspicuously in the fact that these monarchs are no longer concerned about the privilege of burial in the royal necropolis but erect their personal tombs in the vicinity of their own capital cities. The monuments of the princes of the Oryx nome, containing very beautiful col-

62

umned halls, were built near the present village of Beni Hasan. One of these tombs, constructed during the first half of the Twelfth Dynasty (about 1900 B.C.), has a decoration depicting a caravan of thirty-seven Semites delivering precious eye-paint from their homeland in the south of Palestine. When this scene first became known almost a century ago, it was thought by many to represent the arrival of Jacob and his sons. Historical facts, however, preclude this interpretation. The subject-matter is in reality rather one of the many immigrations of eastern Bedouin, common to ancient Egypt.

It was the bold policy of Amen-em-hēt I and his immediate successors not to interfere with the independence of the feudal lords but rather to invest them with full authority in their nomes, thus keeping them loyally attached to the throne. After all, the princes raised taxes for the court, and merited royal praise "when in every year of the cattle-levy" the taxes were delivered punctually and without arrears. And whenever the king needed soldiers, the militias of the nomarchs formed a substantial part of the royal army. Ameny, the ruler of the Oryx nome under Sen-Wosret I, for instance, prides himself that he supplied the king with troops when he "went southward to overthrow his enemies in Kush (Nubia)," and that he later brought four hundred of his best men to the crown prince "when this one undertook an expedition to the gold mines of Nubia."

Gradually, however, the power of the crown increased, and the privileges of the provincial rulers found their proportionate limitation. Another absolutism triumphs over the feudal system. Under Sen-Wosret III, barely a hundred years after Amen-em-hēt ascended the throne, the independence of the nomarchs has disappeared and the bureaucracy of the Pyramid Age is re-established, though not in its old form. The evil experiences of the past were seemingly not forgotten. Instead of the royal retinue which had once caused internal disintegration, it is now the all-powerful bodyguard of the pharaoh which attains ever greater prominence with generous endowments of land, slaves, and bondsmen.

▲ ▲

The relationship of Egypt to her neighbors in the West and in the North, the Libyans as well as the settled or nomadic peoples of the Sinai peninsula and southernmost Palestine, was with few interruptions as peaceful as in the Old Kingdom. The wars that came to pass were more or less marauding or punitive campaigns. There was no thought of imposing a permanent rule over the defeated countries once they had been ravaged and the plunder was carried home to Egypt. With the minor princes

63

in the interior of Palestine and Syria whose lands "were rich in figs, wine, honey, oil, fruit trees, corn, and cattle," traveling merchants—and occasionally a mission from the pharaoh—kept the desired contact. The goods they carried and exchanged may have spread the only knowledge of the political power and the great culture which the empire on the Nile enjoyed.

Quite different was the situation along the seaboard in coastal cities like Gaza, Tyre, Sidon, Byblos, and Ugarit (Ras Shamra). They were ruled by prince-kings who, through shipping and trade, had accumulated great wealth and could afford to adopt the benefits of Egyptian culture in an ever-increasing measure. Even in the Pyramid Age seaworthy ships were plying from Egypt to Byblos, engaged in the exchange of fine ointments and oils, wares of her craftsmen, and articles of personal adornment, for cedars of Lebanon and other Syrian woods which Egypt badly needed in the manufacture of fine cabinet work, furniture, coffins, and for the embalming of mummies. The high esteem in which Egyptian art was held in the Near East is borne out by the fact that its style and technique were imitated by the native work-men of Syria.

Yet the Egyptians had not established any firm control over the coastal cities, although certain princes may have been forced into a state of virtual vassalage to the pharaohs who held monopoly over foreign trade.

The foreign policy of the Amen-em-hēts and Sen-Wosret's toward the countries of the Upper Nile was of an entirely different character. While the Old Kingdom fol-lowed the principles of pacification, content to make the borders and trade routes secure, Egypt was now bent upon actual conquest and subsequent colonization of that region. A displacement of the original population had probably taken place in the Upper Nile valley as early as the Sixth Dynasty. An African people, related to the prehistoric Egyptians but with a strong admixture of negro blood, had penetrated into Lower Nubia and established themselves there. In origin probably nomadic shepherds, they soon became settlers in the Upper Nile valley and developed a culture of their own.

In place of the poor Nubian chieftains of the Old Kingdom, rich princes now ruled; in place of thinly populated and culturally backward communities, there were now prosperous villages owning numerous herds of cattle and fertile fields which held a great attraction for the Egyptians. In addition, they coveted undis-turbed possession and exploitation of the profitable gold mines in the eastern desert. But, above all, Lower Nubia had inestimable value for the royal treasury as the

64

only land of transit for the African trade in ebony, ivory, gold, leopard skins, ostrich feathers, and resin. It had special economic and strategic importance as the terminus of the main caravan roads from the Libyan desert and the Sudan.

By the end of the Eleventh Dynasty, the fight for the subjugation of Lower Nubia, the "miserable land of Kush" as the Egyptians called it, had started. It was continued under Amen-em-hēt I and was brought to its successful conclusion under Sen-Wosret III. The entire land south of the cataract above Wadi Halfa was conquered and the boundary line fixed at Semna. "Whoever of my sons," the king admonishes his successors, "will maintain the boundary stela which My Majesty has erected, is going to be my true son; he is begotten by My Majesty . . . but he who permits it to be overthrown and does not fight for it, is not my son and was not begotten of me."

The newly acquired territory was secured by fortresses at the most important points all the way from the cataracts of Aswan in the North to Semna in the South. Their ruins have survived, and many of them have been examined by the American Harvard-Boston Expedition with a goodly yield of valuable historical and archaeological information.

The development of Egypt's political power was accompanied by a new flowering of art and literature. However, the temples which the pharaohs of the Middle Kingdom had built in the Fayyum, at Koptos, or in Thebes, did not survive. They had already fallen into ruins during the succeeding period of political turmoil, though later replaced by new structures for which in many instances their remains were used as foundations. Today the older sanctuaries have been salvaged by excavations—as for instance at Karnak, Medamud, and Tod (Upper Egypt)—so that we have a rather good idea of the architecture and especially the relief sculpture of the Middle Kingdom. At Karnak, such a great number of fragments was unearthed that it was possible to reconstruct a small sanctuary of Sen-Wosret I in its entirety. The tomb monument of Mentu-hotpe at Deir el Bahri and the mortuary temples at the pyramids of Lisht, excavated by the Metropolitan Museum of New York, show clearly how far new architectural thoughts had been developed and how much of the old heritage was still retained.

The sculpture of the Middle Kingdom stands on the same high level as that of the Pyramid Age. Yet the five centuries which separate the two periods of achievement had not elapsed without leaving their distinct imprint. The dismal civil wars through which the country had to live, coupled with the distress and privation which common people and princes alike had to endure, engendered a serious outlook on life and tinged it with pessimism. While the art of the Pyramid Age portrayed a simple, carefree people, unfraught with problems, their images now divulge the heavy heart of the individual and his sad experiences.

One of the masterpieces of this new realistic art is the superb diorite Sphinx with the portrait-head of Sen-Wosret III in the Metropolitan Museum of New York. The general impressiveness of the broad, bony face with deep wrinkles under the eyes and with drawn mouth is but little impaired by the missing heavy nose. Nor do the disproportionately large ears typical of all statues of this period, or the extremely large royal beard diminish its spiritual quality and aesthetic values.

The wall reliefs and paintings in the rock-tombs of Upper Egypt, though replete with interesting subject-matter, are of no great artistic importance. But there are examples of animal portraiture which compare most favorably with the best ever accomplished in that field.

The period of Sen-Wosret also attained a height in the goldsmith's art never again to be equaled. The pieces of jewelry made by the artists of his day surpass by far both in quality of workmanship and purity of design the much praised gold work of Tut-ankh-Amūn. They are a credit to their creators as well as to their wearers, for only a people of extreme culture could display so much taste and so great an appreciation. Most of this jewelry, found in the tombs of the princesses at the pyramids of Dahshur and Lahun, now graces the museum in Cairo and the Metropolitan Museum of New York.

Literature, too, reached a new climax in the Twelfth Dynasty although it is not unlikely that a part of it was created during the preceding, darker days of the Heracleopolitan kings.

The writings of this period were prized by the Egyptians as gems and constantly copied as "classics" in the schools for scribes. It is for this reason that they have been preserved—many of them in more than one manuscript. Both poetry and prose are represented. Poetry distinguishes itself from prose chiefly by a more fastidious and delicate style of expression. Most poems further exhibit a peculiar form of verse which progresses in a definite rhythm. The entire composition is generally marked by a feature familiar to the student of Hebrew poetry and commonly known as "parallelism of members." A particular thought expressed by certain words in one line is repeated in different words, or else elaborated in a second and sometimes even in a third paralleling line.

In the field of belles-lettres, novel-like tales relating divers adventures in a simple tenor enjoyed great popularity. Some of them are reminiscent of the stories told in

66

the Arabian Nights. Among the didactic treatises, of which the Egyptians of all times were singularly fond, the most admired book was the "Instructions of Amen-em-hēt I." It comprises the literary testament of this great pharaoh who had earned only ingratitude for the good he had achieved for his country. In bitter disappointment, he offers this somber advice to his son and successor:

"Hearken to what I say to thee
   That thou mayest be King of the earth;
   That thou mayest be ruler of the lands;
   That thou mayest increase good.
   Harden thyself against all subordinates.
   The people heed but him who terrorizes them.
   Do not approach them alone.
   Fill not thy heart with a brother.
   Know not a friend.
   Nor make for thyself intimates,
   Wherein there is no end.
   When thou sleepest, guard thine heart thyself,
   For a man has no people
   In days that are evil."

There is not much left of secular poetry to be quoted. Of the hymns to the king, however, a brief sample may be given in the following stanzas from an enthusiastic song composed by an unknown court poet in praise of Sen-Wosret III. The hymn is permeated by genuine sentiment and replete with pleasant similes. It also shows the well elaborated form of the "parallelism of members." The king is greeted by the population as he enters his city and residence:

"Twice great is the king of his city, above a million of arms; as for other rulers, they are but common folk.
Twice great is the king of his city; he is like a dike holding the stream of waters at the time of flood.
Twice great is the king of his city; he is like a cool lodge that lets everybody repose until daylight.
Twice great is the king of his city; he is like a place of refuge that bars the marauder.
Twice great is the king of his city; he is like an asylum shielding the terrified from the enemy.

67

Twice great is the king of his city; he is like a shade, the cool vegetation of the flood at harvest time.

Twice great is the king of his city; he is like a nook that is warm and dry in the days of winter.

Twice great is the king of his city; he is like a rock that bars the tempest when it is stormy weather.

Twice great is the king of his city; he is like Sakhmet (the goddess of war) to the enemy who sets foot over the boundaries."

The major part of Egyptian literature of this period is of the religious type. Most outstanding in this category are two large collections of texts known to scholars as the "Coffin Texts" and "The Book of the Dead." The name "Coffin Texts" was chosen because these writings were found on walls of coffins from the Ninth to the Twelfth Dynasty. In contrast to the older Pyramid Texts which had been written for the benefit of the kings, they were composed in the interest of those who were not of royal blood. The Texts consist of incantations for protection against hunger, thirst, and the many dangers of the Nether World, as well as invocations for assisting the deceased in the continued enjoyment of his earthly associates and pastimes.

The "Book of the Dead," the most famous work of Egyptian religious literature, is similar in scope. Though composed at the end of the Middle Kingdom, it contains quite a number of pieces from very ancient times. The claim of Egyptian tradition to the effect that certain chapters originated in the days of Usaphais (First Dynasty) and Men-kaw-Rē seems to be well justified.

The "Book of the Dead" is preserved in numerous papyrus manuscripts. The latest, most complete ones—often comprising as many as 190 chapters—were written in the last centuries B.C. during the Ptolemaic era. The most beautiful copies, however, were made during the Eighteenth and Nineteenth Dynasties; these are admirably written and lavishly illustrated with so-called "vignettes."

Like the Pyramid and the Coffin Texts, the "Book of the Dead" is not a congruous literary work but a rather haphazardly compiled collection of texts whose number differs with the various copies. Its Egyptian title is "Egress by Day," an appellation actually befitting only the Seventeenth Chapter which empowers the deceased to "egress" from his tomb at sunrise and to return to it at night. This chapter is one of the very oldest parts of the book—so old in fact that it had to be provided with explanatory notes to aid the Egyptian priests no longer able to understand its full meanings.

68

Of equally ancient origin seems to be the Sixty-fourth Chapter, supposedly found by a chief-architect in the days of Usaphais. It represents a condensation of the essential contents of the entire "Book of the Dead."

The most important text is contained in Chapter 125 which in several sections deals with the "Judgment of the Dead." Its main part, entitled "Chapter of Entering into the Hall of Truth," has a vignette illustrating the "Weighing of the Heart." Under a baldachin, Osiris is enthroned with his sisters Isis and Nephthys at his side. The deceased is led into the center of the hall by the jackal-headed god of the dead, Anubis. There the heart of the dead is being weighed by the symbol of truth and justice. A jackal-headed god is also in charge of the scale, while the ibis-headed Thot (Hermes) records the judgment on a sheet of papyrus. If the scale finds the dead wanting, his heart will be cast to the "Devourer of the Dead," a ferocious beast lurking near the scale; in other words, the reward is eternal damnation. If, on the other hand, the heart is found right, then the dead will be brought before Osiris who is ready to receive him into his realm.

Another part of the same chapter depicts Osiris as the Judge of the Dead. In this guise, he is aided by a college of forty-two judges who are terrifying demons with such frightful names as "Devourer of Shadows," "Bone-Crusher," and "Blood-Eater." The dead must make forty-two confessions before these judges to vindicate himself of an equal number of crimes. These are what Egyptologists term the "negative confessions": "I did not rob"; "I did not steal"; "I did not diminish the measure"; "I did not take away food"; "I did not take milk from the mouth of children"; "I did not speak any lies"; "I did not commit adultery"; "I was not deaf to a word of truth"; "I did not revile the king"; "I did not abuse the gods," etc.

If the dead succeeds in his self-vindication, there is no further obstacle to his entry into the Great Beyond. The Egyptian conception of this Beyond, the Elysian fields, is illustrated by the vignette for Chapter 110. It is a farm—the "Field of Reeds," as the Egyptian called it—the peasants' ideal of a homestead. Just as in life, he is represented as a peasant ploughing, sowing, reaping his harvest, and driving his oxen in the tread-mill.

Related to the "Weighing of the Heart" is another chapter—the Thirtieth—supposedly found by a son of King Khufu—entitled "Chapter of Preventing a Man's Heart from Turning against Him in the Nether World." The dead addressed his heart with these words:

"Oh heart of mine, that I have from my mother, do not rise against me; do not tell lies about me before the weighing master."

69

This same incantation was also frequently engraved on the flat surface of large scarabs, placed with the mummies as a precautionary substitute for the heart in case the real one had somehow been lost.

The Sixth Chapter contains a conjuration of the so-called "shawabti" figures, statuettes also put into the tomb with the dead. They are summoned "to do the work of a man in the Nether World."

"Oh statuette, if I am called; if I am counted to do any work that needs be done in the Nether World . . . then thou shalt count thyself in my stead at all times, and in my stead cultivate the fields, fill the canals, and transport sand from the East to the West, just as if thou be the one who was counted to do his duty. Then, thou shalt exclaim and answer: 'It is I! . . . Here I am.' "

Numerous are the "Words of Transfiguration," particularly in Chapters 77 and 88, by which the dead or rather his soul was given the ability to transform himself into all kinds of birds—swallow, hawk, ibis, phoenix—or into a serpent, a crocodile, or a lotus-flower. These transformations, however, are not in the least related to any of the doctrines of metempsychosis or transmigration of souls preached by the Orphic sect, the Pythagoreans, or the philosophers of Eastern India. In contrast to Egyptian concepts, all these doctrines teach that the soul must pass through several stages of purification in its migration from body to body or incarnation to incarnation.

There are also a number of magic formulae whose application permits the dead to pass unhindered through the doors of the Beyond, protecting him lest an enemy wrest head or mouth or heart from him.

The Forty-fifth Chapter, differing from the rest, contains quotations from hymns by which the Egyptian used to greet the sun-god in morning and evening prayers. They were already part of the Pyramid Texts, but the "Book of the Dead" made them more conveniently readable. Among them is the following hymn to the Sun:

"Pay reverence to the Sun-God when he rises
    At the Eastern Horizon of heaven.
    Hail to you who rise
    From the ocean of heaven;
    Who give light to the Two Lands (Egypt, i.e., the world)
    After you have risen.
    Praise to you! (exclaims) the ninefold divinity (of Heliopolis).

    We have raised him with his two royal serpents,
    Him, the beautiful, the beloved youth.

70

When he rises, man lives, and the people cheer him;
The souls of Heliopolis jubilate,
And the souls of Pe and Nekhen (the oldest capitals of Egypt)
Praise him.

Pay reverence to him! say the baboons (who shriek at sunrise).
Praise to you! cry all animals in unison.
The serpent on your brow smites your foe
So that you may rejoice in your (sun)boat.
And happy is your crew.
The bark of day (the boat in which the sun-god sails the skies by day)
Receives you who are of cheerful mood.

Oh Lord of gods, those whom you created
Sing praise to you.
Nut (the goddess of Heaven) is azure at your side;
The Ocean of Heaven (the god Nun) embraces you
With his radiant rays.

Give light to me, too,
So that I may see your beauty.
Happy I was on earth.
I prayed at the sight of your glorious face
When it rose upon the heaven's horizon.
I revered the disk of the sun
When it sank beyond the hills
Of the (western) necropolis.

You unfold yourself when you rise
From the heaven's ocean.
You rejuvenate yourself
Where there was yesterday.
Oh, you divine youth,
You are your own creator; you appear
In the splendor of your own.
Heaven and earth are made light by you.

You are the giver of law
To all the world;
Even the gods say their prayers to you."

Another hymn, in the very same chapter of the "Book of the Dead," sings the praises of the sun-god as "the Living God, the Lord of Love by whose rays each and everybody lives." It reads:

"Lord of Heaven, Lord of the Earth,
King of Justice, Lord of Eternity,
Ruler of the Infinite, Prince over all gods,
Living God who created Eternity,
Who made the heaven
And gave himself a place upon it;
The gods rejoice at your rising,
And the earth is jubilant
At the sight of your radiant glory.
People gather and gaze,
Enraptured, at your beauty,
When you travel the heavens,
Day after day."

These quotations may prove that the "Book of the Dead" is, as James Breasted rightfully stated, "not exclusively a magical vade mecum for use in the here-after," but also disseminates a moral philosophy—though be it a simple one. To be sure, it is far from being an epitome of ethics or deep philosophical thought. Nor does it represent a compendium of Egyptian theology. Those who choose to call it the "Egyptian Bible" truly overestimate its spiritual values.

▲ ▲

The splendor of the Twelfth Dynasty continued to shine down through the centuries, and the memory of its mighty kings lived on. The story of the greatness of Sen-Wosret became a legend which passed into the minds of the Greeks. They saw in Sen-Wosret, as later in Alexander the Great, a world conqueror and a hero possessed with supernatural powers. Whatever Egypt had accomplished in war and peace was attributed to him, and his deeds were incredibly exaggerated. Diodoros, for instance,

72

takes Sen-Wosret in his ventures as far as Thrace, and then beyond to the banks of the Ganges.

For two centuries, the Twelfth Dynasty governed a happy Egypt. Its auspicious rule was even maintained a few decades longer by kings of another line. Then internal troubles arose and, worst of all, conquest by barbarian invaders menaced the very existence of the state. Manetho briefly describes the fateful event that came to pass about 1730 B.C., two hundred and seventy years after the accession of the Twelfth Dynasty, as follows:

"At that time a god became hostile, and unexpectedly men of ignoble birth came from the eastern borders with sufficient boldness to make an expedition into the country, and conquered it easily without even a fight, overpowering those who were ruling there."

Manetho calls the foreigners "Hyksos" or "Shepherd kings." This name, however, is a creation of popular etymology. "Hyksos" is actually a term derived from the Egyptian *"heqew kheswet,"* which means "Ruler of the foreign countries."

Race, origin, and character of the invaders are not definitely ascertainable. The only established fact is that they were not a homogeneous people, though probably composed in the main of Semites, augmented by members of Hurrian stock and descent from Northern Mesopotamia and Syria.

The chief stronghold of the Hyksos was the fortress of Avaris on the eastern borders of Egypt, in the immediate vicinity of the Tanis of later years. Their power expanded to Middle Egypt, and for a time their kings resided in Memphis. Yet they failed to subjugate Upper Egypt. In and around Thebes native princes continued their rule and persisted in their independence as "Kings of Upper Egypt."

On the other hand, the Hyksos gained mastery over Palestine and Syria. They occupied the most important cities of that region, fortified them, and made the native princes tributary. Despite many archaeological finds in Palestine readily attributed to the Hyksos, the details of their rule have remained very inexact. It is still a matter of grave doubt and controversy as to whether there ever existed a greater and united Hyksos empire, allegedly embracing all countries from Middle Egypt to Syria with Avaris as its central capital. It may definitely be assumed, though, that the old trade relations between Egypt and the Near East were not only continued but energetically fostered.

The Hyksos left but few reminders of their rule in Egypt: mainly scarabs bearing strange designs or corruptions of names and titles of their kings. They never developed any cultural life of their own. Accordingly, no foundation in fact can be established for the assumption that they acquainted Egypt with the alloy of copper and tin (bronze), or that they were masters of the art of working in metals.

As five hundred years earlier after the collapse of the Old Kingdom, the struggle for the reuniting of the "Two Lands" was started once more from Thebes. The war of liberation from the Hyksos was begun by King Seken-en-Rē. He was probably killed in action, for his mummy shows a fatal wound in the forehead. His son Ka-mose continued the fight until his early death, after which his brother Ah-mose carried the war to a victorious conclusion. After a long and tedious siege, the fortress of Avaris was taken; the Hyksos warriors withdrew to Palestine and Syria where they were welcomed by related princes. In order to forestall any attempts at renewed invasion, Ah-mose pursued them with his victorious troops. He besieged the city of Sharuhen in Southern Palestine, where part of the Hyksos forces had entrenched themselves, and finally captured it after three years. Thus Egypt was delivered from the "plague" and again became a free country.

Nevertheless, the Egyptians owed their invaders a debt of gratitude. Through them, they made an acquisition foreign to the land of the Nile, but destined to play an important role as vehicle of war and means of transportation for the nobility: horse and chariot. There is little doubt that the enemy accomplished his easy victory as much through the employment of his "cavalry" as by the use of his newly fashioned bronze scimitar.

The horse and, with it, the chariot had probably been brought to Syria by the Hurrians at an earlier date. Egypt, however, credited the Semite Hyksos with the importation, and took the words for horse ("ses-met," the Hebraic "sus") and chariot ("merkobte," the Hebraic "merkaba") into its vocabulary from their language.

▲　▲

The Jewish writer Josephus, born in 37 A.D., virtually identified the Hebrews with the Hyksos. Modern historians have followed suit, basing their convictions on the story of the sojourn of the children of Israel in the land of the pharaohs and their ultimate exodus. Further credence is lent to this "identification" theory by the account given in Genesis 46, 6; "And they took their cattle and their goods, which they had gotten in the land of Canaan, and came into Egypt, Jacob and all his seed with him." Nothing in Egyptian records, however, gives any indication that Hebrews and Hyksos were actually one and the same.

The Biblical tradition may nonetheless contain a kernel of historical truth.

74

There is some possibility or even probability that, at one time or another, Hebrew tribes had come from Canaan to Egypt and left again after a prolonged stay; or that there were Hebrew clans living among the Hyksos. Certain dim recollections of such happenings may have been absorbed by the Biblical tradition. This whole rather difficult problem was last treated in "Egypt and the Old Testament" (Liverpool and London, 1932)—a work of critical astuteness and comprehensiveness by the late Egyptologist T. Eric Peet. Whatever final analysis may reveal, as far as Egyptian history is concerned, the event was of but minor importance.

75

New Kingdom

1546-1350

XVIII Dynasty 1546–1350 B.C.

IV

THEBES

The conquest of the Hyksos by King Ah-mose marks the dawn of another era in Egyptian history. It heralds the five imperialistic centuries of the New Kingdom during which pharaonic rule covered all Egypt, the Sudan, and a large part of the Near East.

Amen-hotpe I, the son of Ah-mose, and his successor, Thut-mose I, were the founders of the empire which had no less brilliant representatives in the consecutive kings of the Eighteenth Dynasty who bore the same names.

Their first and foremost task consisted in healing the many wounds inflicted upon the kingdom of Sen-Wosret by the Asiatic invaders; in "restoring that which lay in ruins; in building up that which was unfinished; and, since the Asiatics had been in Avaris in the Northland (Delta), in overthrowing that which had been done while they ruled in ignorance of Rē."

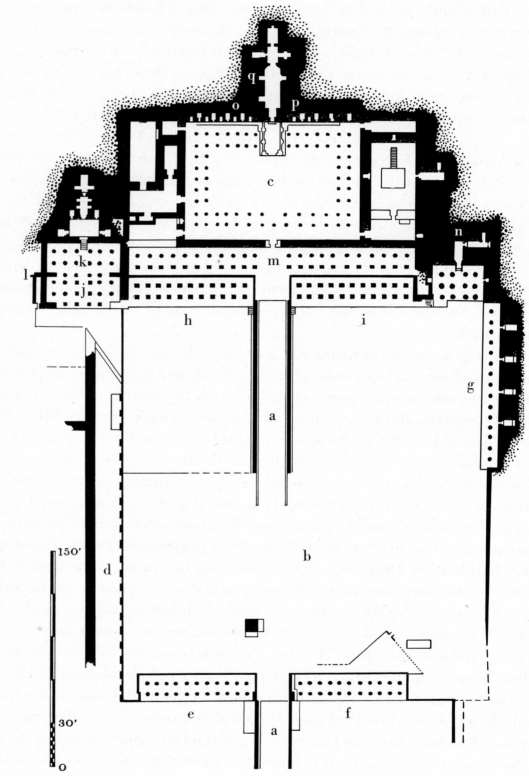

TEMPLE OF
DEIR EL BAHARI

a Ascent
b Central Court
c Upper Court
d Supporting Wall
e S. Colonnade
f N. Colonnade
g Unfinished Colonnade
h Punt Colonnade
i Birth Colonnade
j I. Colonnade
k II. Colonnade
l Shrine of Hathor
m Granite Door
n Chapel of Anubis
o Recesses
p Recesses
q Sanctuary

Minor uprisings within the country and abroad had to be suppressed. The southern region between the cataracts had to be regained. A successful military expedition penetrated "through valleys no one had traversed before," the Sudan as far as Napata, a city at the foot of the "Holy Mountain," the Gebel Barkal. The borders of Egypt were extended, and a new and productive province added to its territory. It was given an administration of its own, headed by a viceroy, the "Viceroy of Kush."

In Asia, Thut-mose I drove victoriously through Palestine and Syria, as far as the banks of the Euphrates, but did not establish control over the conquered lands.

It is recorded that the pharaoh, during this "triumphant campaign," not only "threw his foe" but in the land of Niy on the upper Euphrates captured elephants "the like of which was never seen before by any king." Thut-mose took the precious tusks back to Egypt as trophies, and donated them to the Amūn temple of Karnak. This ancient place of worship was also favored by other royal deeds of "charity." The king presented it with a "magnificent hall of papyrus columns, and erected in front of its pylon two tall obelisks of red granite," one of which still points proudly to the zenith.

Strong as the ruling house was, it was beset by intrigues of a type rather common in oriental courts. To disentangle their threads and to identify the personalities involved in their lengthy plots constitute a task beyond the ability of even the most astute historian. But a few facts may be established with certainty. When Thut-mose I died in about 1520 B.C., he was succeeded by a son named Thut-mose II who, born of a subordinate wife, was not entitled to the throne. In strict conformity with the laws of succession, the crown should have passed to an older half-sister of his, Hatshepsut who was the daughter of Thut-mose I and a real princess, a "Great Royal Wife." In order to avoid dynastic complications and to satisfy the orthodox legitimists at court, no better plan could have been devised than to have Hat-shepsut marry her half-brother Thut-mose, thus legitimizing his claims to the throne. Despite the close relationship, this union was not regarded as abnormal by the Egyptians.

Unfortunately, this marriage remained childless, and the sickly young king decided to adopt a son, also called Thut-mose, and to appoint him as his successor. The descent of this third Thut-mose cannot be exactly determined. He, too, may have been a son of Thut-mose I and a half-brother of Hat-shepsut and Thut-mose II; or he may have been a son of the second Thut-mose and some subordinate wife of his. In any case, when Thut-mose II died after a rather short reign, the young Thut-mose III became king, and the dowager queen Hat-shepsut assumed the regency for the years of his minority. It is more than likely that she raised the boy-king to the

status of her husband in order to entrench herself more firmly in the regency. Whatever means she chose, the fact remains that she succeeded in pushing the king completely into the background. When Thut-mose III became of age, Hat-shepsut refused to surrender the regency and usurped the titles of the sovereign ruler of Egypt.

While inscriptions refer to Hat-shepsut as a woman, she is represented—in pictures, statues, and sphinxes—not in the attire of a queen but in the traditional vestment of the king: short kilt and stylized beard.

Hat-shepsut was, no doubt, a most intelligent and strong-willed woman. However, it was her particularly good fortune that she had in Sen-Mūt, the leader of the legitimist party, a chancellor of equal energy who fostered her love of power and assisted her in the execution of her ambitious plans. Of simple origin, this Sen-Mūt had as a youth entered into the service of the Amūn Temple of Karnak and was soon promoted to a number of important offices. How his acquaintance with the queen developed, how he won her favor, and perhaps her love, is nowhere recorded. It has been confirmed, though, that Hat-shepsut made him tutor of her daughter Nefru-Rē and bestowed upon him honors, "the like of which were not to be found in the writings of the ancestors."

Egypt prospered during the twenty-one years of Hat-shepsut's reign. Of great economic importance was a trading expedition she sent to the distant land of Punt, which may be identical with the Somali Coast of East Africa. The most valuable product of this country was incense—from time immemorial a prime essential for Egyptian temple services. The god Amūn himself had commanded the queen: "Seek out the roads to Punt, and open the paths to the land of myrrh." Thus five great ships were fitted out and sailed from Thebes, downstream through a canal to Suez, and thence into the Red Sea. They weighed anchor near the groves of incense trees, in a country quite different from the familiar Nile Valley. The Egyptians brought the products of their homeland: articles of personal adornment, weapons, and many foods that were undoubtedly rare and a most welcome delicacy to the barbarians. In exchange they received great quantities of incense, gold, ebony, elephant tusks, live leopards and monkeys, and even incense trees planted in tubs. The flotilla returned heavily laden with treasures, "the like of which had never been brought to other kings."

Hat-shepsut erected magnificent temples in Thebes and other cities. But following the example of her father Thut-mose, her first consideration was for the sanctuary of Karnak. She once said of herself that "she could not sleep on account of this temple." The halls, courts, and twin seventy-foot obelisks bear witness to her devo-

tion. The obelisks, monoliths of red granite, were cut and finished in the quarries of Aswan—an immense task requiring seven full months. Boats, especially constructed for the purpose, carried them to Thebes where they were finally set up in the temple. "There," it is said, "they mingled with the heavens," and their tips, encased in the purest gold, let "their rays flood over Egypt; and when the sun rises between them, it is as though it rose on the Eastern horizon."

The great masterpiece among the buildings of Hat-shepsut is the terrace temple on the western banks of the Nile at Thebes, known today as the temple of Deir el Bahri or the "Northern Monastery." Its plan was probably designed and executed by Sen-Mūt who may have preferred his accomplishments as "Chief Architect" to his political pursuits. The monument he erected to the glory of his royal mistress and his own person ranks with the best works of Egyptian architecture. It occupies a place of honor made doubly secure by the excavations and restorations which the Egyptian Expedition of the Metropolitan Museum of New York carried on during a period of twenty years of constant effort (1911 to 1931); since 1921, under the leadership of Herbert E. Winlock who has given an extremely engaging and vivid account of this work in his book, "Excavations at Deir el-bahri" (New York, 1942).

The temple was dedicated to Amūn, the king of the gods, the queen's "divine father." But there were also chapels devoted to Hathor, the cow-goddess, who had supposedly nursed Hat-shepsut "with sweet milk," and to Anubis, the god of the dead. Several chambers served the mortuary cult of the queen and her parents.

The sun-god Rē-Harakhte also had his place of worship: an open court with an altar where morning and evening a priest recited a hymn in praise of the celestial body.

With astonishing ingenuity, the architect mastered the problems presented by the very nature of the building site itself. Into the semicircle of declining mountains, closed off by precipitous rocks, he nestled his structure in three terraces. The resplendent white of the limestone blocks of which the temple walls are built stands out beautifully against the light brown and golden yellow of the hillsides: a color scheme most certainly not accidental but created by the imagination of an artist-architect.

Flanked by sphinxes, a processional causeway leads from below to the entrance of the sanctuary. Each of the terrace courts is connected with the others by ramps; each is bounded by a pillared hall ornate with Osiride statues of the queen and with series of magnificent reliefs. Two of these series glorify the famed trade expedition to the land of Punt and the mysterious genesis and birth of Queen Hat-shepsut;

89

others depict processions of priests and officials laden with offerings. In view of so much splendor, Hat-shepsut was indeed fully justified in naming this temple "Magnificent is the Magnificence of Amūn."

Thut-mose III, the shadow king, resented the unrestricted domination of "Pharaoh" Hat-shepsut and Chancellor Sen-Mūt. He bided his time, and his time came. He rid himself of his chief opponent Sen-Mūt, and of the clique of hangers-on upon whose support the rule of Hat-shepsut had depended. The queen managed to cling to the throne for a while longer, but soon died in 1479 B.C.—of what may well be regarded as unnatural causes.

Thut-mose, still a comparatively young man of forty, became sole ruler of the state. The full weight of his pent-up hatred fell upon the woman who had done all she could to eliminate him and to make his life miserable. He gave orders to wipe out all memories of her, to destroy her images and erase her name wherever found so that, according to Egyptian belief, her existence in the hereafter would be annihilated. His vengeance was wreaked of course upon the temple of Deir el Bahri as well. If the sanctuary had not been formally dedicated to the cult of Amūn, he would probably have demolished it completely. As it was, only the sphinxes and statues of the queen were smashed to pieces and thrown into a deserted quarry—where they remained until Herbert Winlock discovered them. He succeeded in piecing together the many fragments of her portraits which are now in the Metropolitan Museum of New York. Thus the memories of the persecuted queen have been restored, and her "happy existence" in the hereafter may have been given renewed life.

Thut-mose III ranks as the great warrior among the pharaohs. Upon the foundations laid down by Thut-mose I, he was able to build the empire and secure Egypt's position as the dominating power in the Near East. But he accomplished his task not without bitter contest. The hardest battle he had to win occurred soon after he took over the government. The princes of Kadesh on the Orontes river had formed an alliance with Syrian princes "to the ends of the earth," dedicated to armed resistance against any attempt of the pharaoh to bring their lands under Egyptian sovereignty. However, Thut-mose's art of war broke the combined opposition in a great battle before the walls of Megiddo. Soon after, the city itself, the main enemy-stronghold, had to surrender; the defeat of the enemy became an acknowledged fact.

In ensuing campaigns Thut-mose conquered the countries of Syria and forced their princes to accept Egyptian sovereignty. Major coastal trading cities were taken by the Egyptian fleet. The booty of war supplied "all harbors with fine-bread and other kinds of bread; with beer, wine, honey, and the many fruits of the land . . .

90

the forces of the king were drunk every day, and anointed as on a feast day in Egypt."

Thut-mose immortalized his martial exploits on the walls of the great temple of Karnak. One relief shows the Conqueror as he seizes, symbolically, a mass of Syrian enemies by their hair in order to deal them the deathblow. On the banks of the Euphrates he had a victory stela erected for himself, as his father Thut-mose I had done before him. He also followed his father's example as a huntsman.

A young officer of his army, Amen-em-hāb by name, tells the eye-witness story of how the pharaoh made a kill of one hundred and twenty elephants. When the biggest of the animals charged the king, the officer, with great presence of mind, cut off its trunk and rendered it harmless. As a reward for his bravery, Amen-em-hāb was decorated with a medal of gold. He tells of another exploit by which he rescued the king's army from a precarious situation. When they besieged Kadesh, the native prince used a ruse in order to throw the Egyptian charioteers into confusion. He released a mare from the city to excite the stallions drawing the chariots. When they were just at the point of running away, the quick-witted Amen-em-hāb jumped from his chariot, chased the mare, cut her belly open with a stroke of his sword, and severed her tail—which he presented to His Majesty triumphantly.

Furthermore, Thut-mose III excelled in more than just military affairs. He proved himself to be an exemplary statesman by the inner organization of the empire.

In sharp contrast to the feudalism particularly dominant during the first half of the Middle Kingdom, the Egypt of the Eighteenth Dynasty is a bureaucracy with a centralized government controlling the resources of the entire country. The King, as the greatest landowner and hence possessed of the largest material wealth, is the natural head of the state. The various branches of the administration are under the direction of officials who are solely responsible to the pharaoh. However, with the increase in the size of the army and its ever more important services to the crown, the military gradually gains in influence. The nobility of officials sees itself confronted with a new nobility of soldiers. The still firmly entrenched officials look with misgivings and disdain upon their rivals. This spirit is fostered in the schools for scribes; these scholars are told deterrent stories about the military career and given profound warnings against this profession:

"Do not believe that the soldier is better off than the scribe... When he marches through the Syrian mountains, he must carry his bread and water himself; ... his neck gets as stiff as a donkey's: ... He must drink foul water... When he finally

92

encounters the enemy, he has no more energy left in his bones; . . . And when he returns home, he is like a piece of worm-eaten wood. . ."

These exhortations, of course, were of little or no avail. The king needed his army. A general with his forces was of greater value to him than a secretary of the treasury with a host of even the best trained office-holders.

▲ ▲

When Thut-mose III died in 1461 B.C., he left behind him a kingdom thus far unparalleled in extent and organization. History rightfully dubbed him "The Great." Although from time to time his heirs and successors had to resort to force of arms to subdue rebellions of seditious princes, they were still able to maintain the empire which he had built. Egypt, in general, enjoyed the blessings of enduring peace.

The most brilliant representative of this fortunate era was Amen-hotpe III, the grandson of Thut-mose III, and third in his succession. He epitomizes the magnificent oriental ruler indulging in the very best life has to offer. From the tombs of his great officials, and the archaeological finds which have come to light, the vanished golden age of the Eighteenth Dynasty beckons with the fascination of a fairy tale.

In artistic ideas; in the amazing skill of their technical execution; in culture, even to the details of costume and ornament; in social as well as official life, standards are set that were never again attained. All the achievements of Egyptian genius in the thousand years since the building of the pyramids are embodied in this period.

The Egyptian of the Eighteenth Dynasty led a life of wealth and luxury that was by no means restricted to persons of rank or to high officials. Drudgery in the quarries and mines and all the heavy labor connected with building large temples and rock-tombs for the kings had been delegated to slaves from foreign lands and to prisoners of war. Common citizen and farmer alike were thus able to have a more pleasant existence.

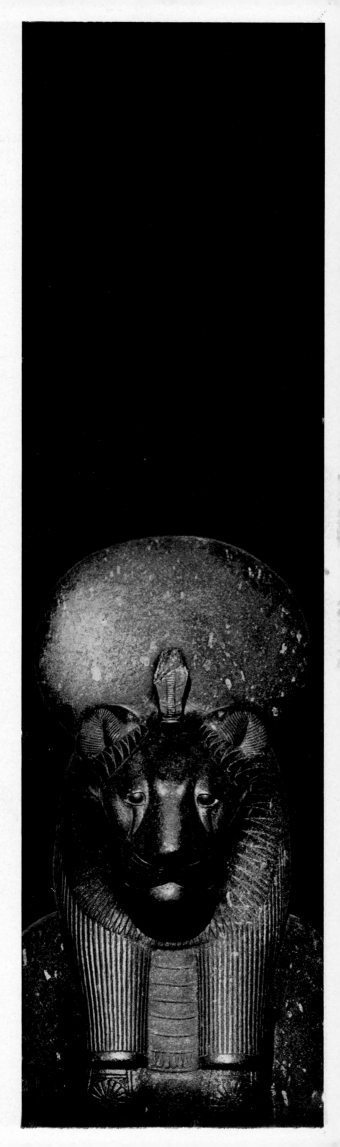

Everywhere palaces and villas displayed exceptional luxury. What is more impressive, however, is the fact that even the homes of commoners had their share of extravagance. The plain household furnishings of their forebears no longer sufficed. The desire for greater magnificence had made itself felt throughout the land.

Architecturally, Thebes, the capital, excelled every other city in Egypt—in fact, any city in the world of that time. This splendor is well attested by the ostentatious royal palaces and grandiose temples within its realm.

The Terrace Temple of Hat-shepsut was but a single example. Another striking one is the great Amūn Temple of Karnak, created by the same Hat-shepsut and Thut-mose III. Today its buildings are a vast field of ruins. Only two tall obelisks and two gigantic granite pillars bearing the heraldic signs of Upper and Lower Egypt, lily and papyrus, remain to tell of its vanished glory.

The "Festival Temple" of Thut-mose III, however, is still preserved. Erected for the occasion of one of his governmental jubilees, it simulates a tent and boasts of a main hall that may well be regarded as the most beautiful interior ever created in Egypt.

The acme of temple architecture was reached in the Amūn sanctuary built by Amen-hotpe III in Luxor. The great court with pillared halls is of unequaled perfection, comparable only to the court of the Tulun Mosque in Cairo, a masterwork of Islamic architecture built between 883 and 886 A.D. Not exactly advantageous to its entire arrangement was the enlargement of the Luxor Temple made by Ramesses II a century later. This addition consisted of a court with royal statues and two towering pylons upon which the pharaoh had his martial exploits immortalized in word and picture.

A mortuary temple of Amen-hotpe III at Thebes, on the western banks of the Nile, has completely disappeared except for two colossal statues—the famous "Colossi of Memnon"—which originally stood in front of it. In the Roman Imperial period they were taken to be statues of Memnon, the son of Eos and Tithonos who had fallen before Troy. Both of them actually represent Amen-hotpe III.

One of the colossi was believed to emit a melodious tone at sunrise. Thus the image would offer sweet and plaintive greeting to his mother Eos as she made her appearance on earth at dawn. The goddess, hearing the sound, would shed her tears, the morning dew, over her beloved son. Many travelers of old claim to have heard the phenomenon. Others, among them the geographer Strabo, doubt its authenticity. The emperor Hadrian (130 A.D.) together with a large retinue spent several days at the "singing" colossus. During his reign, a veritable flood of verses was poured

96

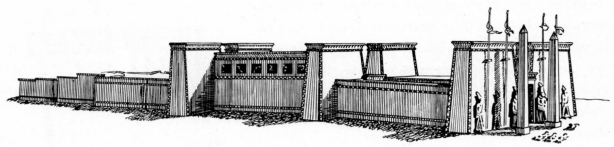

TEMPLE OF AMŪN, LUXOR (RECONSTRUCTION)

out at the feet of the monumental figure. By far the best one, written by a certain Asclepiodotus who identifies himself as "imperial procurator and poet," may be given in the following translation:

"Sea-born Thetis, learn that Memnon never suffered pangs of dying.
  Still, where Libyan mountains rise, sounds the voice of his loud crying
  (Mountains which the Nile-stream, laving, parts from Thebes, the hundred-
      gated)
  When he glows, through rays maternal with warm light illuminated.
  But thy son who, never sated, dreadful battle still was seeking,
  Dumb in Troy and Thessaly, rests now, never speaking."

The strange phenomenon ceased after Septimius Severus (193-211 A.D.) had the upper portion of the colossus restored—perhaps in order to propitiate the angry god. Of the many explanations offered for the miraculous resonance of the stone image, none has ever satisfied men of science.

The colossi are among the greatest of their kind. The height of the figures measures 52 feet; that of the pedestal, upon which their feet are resting, 13 feet. The statues are carved from a pebbly and quartzose sandstone found in the mountains south of Thebes near Edfu. This material is of a yellowish-brown color and most difficult to work.

The predecessors of the Eighteenth Dynasty had pyramidal tombs of brick built for themselves at Thebes, on the western banks of the Nile. Thut-mose I broke with the ancient traditions which dictated that the king's tomb had to be a pyramid. Instead, he chose a rock-tomb hollowed out of the cliffs of an isolated valley in the Libyan mountains—a place which the modern Arabs call Biban el Muluk, or "Tomb Holes of the Kings." Since there was no space in the narrow desert valley for the

104

customary mortuary temple, another innovation became necessary. The mortuary temple had to be separate from the burial-place. Thus it was erected as an independent structure—a "Memorial Temple" in the Nile valley on the narrow strip of desert between the cultivated land and the mountain slopes.

For centuries the example set by Thut-mose was followed by succeeding pharaohs; the lonely desert valley gradually became honeycombed with tombs. Strabo, on his visit to Egypt, reported that there were about forty "royal tombs hollowed out of the rock, magnificently arranged and worth seeing." The majority of these were re-discovered in the nineteenth century; last of all, the now world-famous tomb of Tut-ankh-Amūn in 1922.

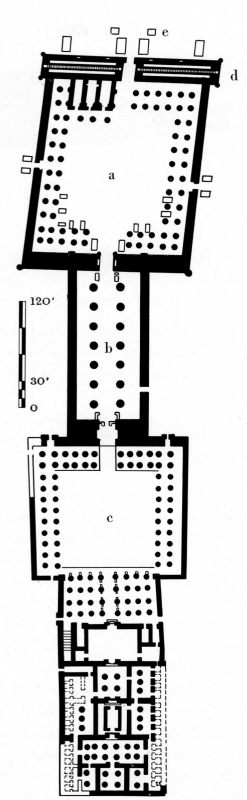

TEMPLE OF AMŪN. LUXOR

a Court of Ramesses II
b Colonnade
c Court of Amen-hotpe III
d Principal Pylon
e Obelisk

120'

30'

0

105

After the great wars of Thut-mose III, Egypt entertained the most favorable relations with foreign countries. The pharaohs maintained constant contact with the rulers of the powerful neighboring kingdoms of Babylonia and Assyria, with Mitani on the Upper Euphrates, the Hittite kingdom in Asia Minor, and the Minoan kingdom of Crete. Communication with the various courts was upheld by ambassadors and emissaries who carried bulky letters and reports, all written on cuneiform tablets in Babylonian—the diplomatic language of the times. The mutual friendship of the monarchs rested principally upon the exchange of presents, consisting of manufactured wares and such precious raw materials as gold. In the guise of such gifts, these kings carried on a rather remunerative trade. Of course, the Egyptian pharaohs liked to call the goods coming from the aliens "tribute" of foreign princes. It was undoubtedly made a great event when such articles arrived at Thebes and were taken over by high officials of the state. The receipt of tribute even became a favorite subject for picturization in the tombs. "Coming from all ends of the earth," foreign dignitaries in characteristic attire are shown humbly bowing and "carrying gifts on the back."

The relationship between the princely houses was further strengthened by marriages—which in turn entailed payment of large dowries representing purchase values "that were without limit and reached from the earth to the heaven."

106

The Religious Revolution

Akh-en-Aten
1375-1350 B.C.

V

EL AMARNEH

Upon the death of Amen-hotpe III after a lingering illness (1375 B.C.), his son Amen-hotpe IV began a reign which steered Egypt into a serious crisis. The youthful king—at this time probably not more than twenty-five or twenty-six years old—at once introduced a new faith. This new "teaching," as he expressed it, was intended to replace the old inherited religion already subjected to many modifications in the course of the centuries.

For over a thousand years, the falcon-headed Rē-Harakhte, who was identified with the sun-god Hor of Heliopolis, had been the undisputedly supreme god of Egypt and the divine protector of the pharaohs. In the beginning of the New Kingdom, however, Thebes became the capital, and Amen-Rē, who had been worshiped there was accordingly made the leading divinity. As sun-god he was invested by the priests with all the attributes originally befitting only Rē-Harakhte. He was credited with being the creator and ruler of the world, the peerless progenitor of all existence. In his name, the great wars in Nubia and Syria were fought and won. In his honor, temples were erected in the conquered countries, and he received the lion's share of all booty. His old sanctuary in Thebes (Karnak) became the temple of the realm. Little wonder, then, that the priesthood of Heliopolis watched the rise of Amūn with envy. They impatiently awaited a chance to dethrone the "King of gods" and to reinstate his predecessor Hor with the old political and religious prerogatives. This opportunity came when Amen-hotpe ascended the throne.

110

Without reservation, the young king proclaimed himself an adherent of the sun-god of Heliopolis. What is more, he went even further. Rē-Harakhte was elevated to supreme deity and given a long mysterious appellation probably not too easily understood even by contemporary Egyptians. Commonly, however, the name of the god was expressed by the simple word "Aten" meaning "Sun-disk."

At first, the cults of the old gods remained in existence. After a few years, however, Aten-worship became the official state religion, and Aten the one and only god. All previous deities were eliminated, and a persecution was vigorously instituted against the Theban Amūn and his kin, the goddess Mūt and the moon-god Khonsu. Their images were destroyed, and their names obliterated wherever found. By the same token, all bearers of personal names compounded with "Amūn" changed their names. Among the first to do so was King Amen-hotpe himself. He renounced his name "Amen-hotpe" meaning "Amūn is satisfied," and henceforth called himself "Akh-en-Aten," or "He is pleasing to the Aten." The traditional forms of worship were likewise discarded. While, in the beginning, the new god was still represented as a falcon-headed man in the same manner as Rē-Harakhte, any such personification was now disdained and all divine images were abolished. Worship was strictly limited to the visible celestial body of the radiant sun, symbolically depicted as a disk with long rays ending in hands. Hymns were sung, and sacrifices were offered upon an altar under the skies—no longer in the darkness of a temple cella.

The Aten religion was a "monotheistic" but rather materialistic creed; in all its essentials, quite distinct and remote from that of the Psalmists, the Prophets or, especially, Christianity. Though the poignant four words of the Gospel of Saint John—Light, Life, Love, and Truth—were constantly emphasized, they did not have the same connotation as that given them by the Evangelist.

Untiring scientific research has penetrated deeply into the nature of the Aten religion which underwent so many purifications during its short life. Yet its innermost essence and undercurrents remain unrevealed. While King Akh-en-Aten undoubtedly was the most zealous protagonist of the new "teaching," there is no definite reason to assume that he was also its spiritual father. On the other hand, it was he who conceived the great hymn expressing, in deep poetic passion and glowing devotion, the might and beauty of Aten; a song of praise that may be considered the very confession of the new faith. Many of its verses are in word and thought repetitive of the old hymns to the sun. But Akh-en-Aten's poem deviates just as frequently from previous ideas about the sun-god and invests Aten, the creator and sustainer of the world, with greater purity of spirit. Insight into the nature of his thinking may

111

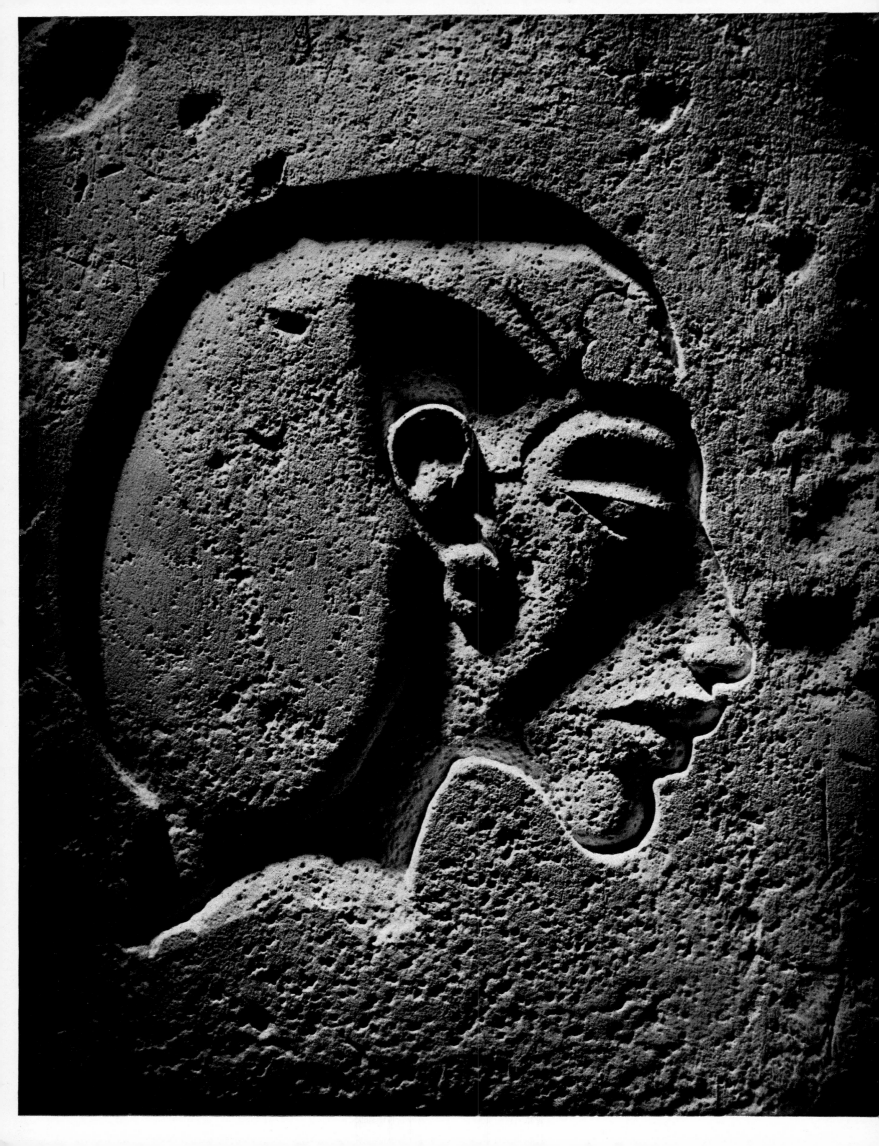

be gained from the following passages of the rather lengthy poem. The selection is based on translations made by this author and, more recently, by Norman de G. Davies and James H. Breasted:

"You appear so full of beauty on the horizon of the skies,
You, living Sun-disk (Aten), that lived before all else.
You rise in the eastern horizon,
You fill every land with your beauty.
You are beauteous and great, glistening high above all lands.
Your rays encompass the lands to the very ends of all that you have made . . .
Though you are far away, your rays are on this earth.
Though you are in the faces of men, your footsteps are not seen.
When you set on the western horizon,
The earth is in darkness as if in death. . ."

Men are seized with fast slumber, and only beasts of prey,
Lions and serpents, come forth from their dens.
But what a change

"When you rise on the horizon, and when you shine,
Sun-disk by day,
You dispel the darkness.
The world is in festivity each day:
Men awaken and stand upon their feet;
They wash their limbs, and put on clothes;
And their arms are raised in prayer,
For you have appeared.
The entire world does its work:
All cattle rest in the pastures;
The trees and plants are green;
The birds are fluttering from their nests,
Wings raised in adoration of you.
The lambs are dancing on their feet,
All creatures that there fly or creep,
They live when you have shone upon them. . ."

And so the sun awakens life in the waters:
"The barks are sailing to and fro, North and South;
The fish in the river swim before you;

Your rays pierce the depth of the great sea..."

The sun is man's creator:
"You create the vital germ in women;
You make the seed in men,
Giving life to the son in his mother's body;
When the child comes forth from his mother's womb
On the day of his birth,
You open his mouth altogether,
You supply his necessities."

The sun is the creator of animals:
"You give the breath of life
To the fledgling in the shell;
He comes forth from the egg to chirp in due time."

And the creator of the Universe is the sun:
"How manifold are your works
(Though) they are hidden before mankind,
O sole God, beside whom there is no other.
You have created the earth after your own desire
With man, and cattle, and all small creatures;
With all that walks upon its feet,
Or flies in the air on its wings;
The land of Syria, and the land of Ethiopia,
And the land of Egypt.
You put everybody where he belongs,
And give him everything he needs.
Everybody has his food (from you),
And his days are numbered (by you).
The tongues of men are different in speech,
And likewise the shapes of men,
And their skins are distinct from each other.
Thus, you divide all peoples...
You make the river Nile in the Nether World,
And send it forth as you desire
To nourish the people of Egypt...

114

All the distant countries, you also make them live.
You have set a heavenly Nile (the rain)
That falls on them;
It makes waves in the mountains,
Watering the fields with as much as they need. . ."

"You have created the seasons, the winter cold,
And the summer heat.
You have created the distant skies to shine in them,
And to behold all that which you have made. . .
You make millions of forms by your own self,
Cities, villages and fields, roads and rivers.
All eyes look upon you when you, Sun-disk, are over the earth by day. . .
The entire world is sustained in your hands. . .
When you have risen, they live;
When you set, they die:
For you are of yourself the length of life;
Man lives through you. . ."

In order to serve his god with the deepest ardor, the king made the final decision. Together with the entire court, he abandoned the capital of Thebes, where everything was traditionally linked with Amūn, and founded a new city. For its site a district was chosen — the present El Amarneh, half-way between Thebes and Memphis.

The new residence was given the name "Horizon-of-the-Sun-disk, Aten," for it was to belong to nobody but him, with its fertile lands, mountains and desert, a "Holy See" within the kingdom of Egypt. Royal palaces and a great temple of Aten, sumptuous villas for the high officials, and extensive administrative buildings were erected. In the eastern hills tombs for the great were laid out and decorated with pictures illustrating primarily the cult of Aten and important court events as well.

There is good reason to assume that the new religion was embraced principally by court and official circles. The people at large probably did not bother too much about it but rather continued in their customary offerings to the old familiar gods. However, those who voluntarily confessed the new "teaching" were rewarded, regardless of their descent, with the highest administrative positions and excellent incomes. Thus a commoner by the name of May, who advanced to leadership in the

116

army of the "Lord of the Two Lands," became "royal scribe." As "fan-bearer on the King's Right," with duties that brought him into intimate personal contact with the king, he could proudly say:

> "How prosperous is he who hearkens to the 'teaching' of Life. I was a man of low origin, both on my father's and my mother's side, but my lord promoted me because I did his teaching, and hearkened incessantly to his voice. He multiplied my favors by the number of grains of sand. He let me grow; he enriched me by his munificence when I was a man of no property; he handed provisions and rations every day to me who had been one that went a-begging for bread."

Light-hearted serenity reigned in El Amarneh in spite of the grave and ardent piety to which Akh-en-Aten held his family and his retinue. He was wholly devoted to his royal wife, the greatly admired and very beautiful Nefret-ity. At her side, he strolled under the shady trees or along the flower-beds of the palace gardens. Together, they played and frolicked with the princesses in the private apartments of the harem. Neither in the temple nor at any festal occasion could the king be seen without his spouse or his daughters. His was an idyllic family life that was seemingly unruffled by care.

The new religion also carried a new art into El Amarneh. Another spirit, a tendency to be natural and honest, expresses itself and becomes most evident in the portraits of the king. He is no longer shown as an idealized demi-god without individual human traits, as the pharaohs of the Eighteenth Dynasty before him had usually been depicted, but true-to-life with all the unseemly peculiarities of face and body.

The splendor of El Amarneh lasted for little more than a decade. Even before the king's death, violent family feuds arose which destroyed the palace idyl of the royal couple. Akh-en-Aten had no male heir. Very much against the will of Queen Nefret-ity, he appointed as his co-regent and successor the young husband of his eldest daughter, Smenkh-ka-Rē, who enjoyed his special favor. In addition, political differences intervened. While the king himself relented in his animosity against Amūn and worked toward a reconciliation with the still-powerful priesthood of Thebes, the queen adhered to the Aten religion with burning fanaticism. Not unlike the ambitious Hat-shepsut a hundred and fifty years before her, she tried to take the reins of the government into her own hand, aided in her designs by a probably large party at the royal court. The intrigues that were plotted, and the controversies that resulted in El Amarneh, are nowhere recorded.

Suddenly and almost simultaneously, Akh-en-Aten and Smenkh-ka-Rē died—in all likelihood not of natural causes. Thereupon, something unheard of in the annals of Egyptian history happened. Nefret-ity addressed herself in a letter to the Hittite king in Asia Minor, perhaps a close relative of hers, to beg him in all seriousness to despatch a prince to become her husband and, through her favor, king of Egypt. The prince was sent but vanished on his voyage. Owing to these circumstances, Nefret-ity's claims to the throne were disregarded once and for all. She disappeared entirely from the scene, and complete mystery shrouds her further fate.

Another son-in-law of Akh-en-Aten, Tut-ankh-Aten—a mere lad of ten—was placed on the throne by a certain General Eye, an old partisan of the heretic pharaoh. Tut-ankh-Aten, however, was forced somehow to return to Thebes and the old religion. He reconciled himself with the proscribed gods, Amūn and his family. Consequently his name was changed to Tut-ankh-Amūn, "Precious of Life of Amūn," by which he is known to history. If it were not for the discovery of his lavishly equipped tomb in 1922, this rather insignificant pharaoh would be of little or no renown. In complete denial of his early past, the youthful monarch prides himself that he "resettled Thebes, made good laws and re-established the old rights, being the beloved son of Amen-Rē, the king of all gods."

Despite all the benevolent tolerance which the king, his counselors and other men behind the throne publicly extended to the old religion and its priests, they could not cleanse their reputation of the stains of their previous intimate relationship with the El Amarneh cult.

Tut-ankh-Amūn occupied the throne for nine years. He was succeeded by General Eye whose rather brief rule was unable to restore internal peace in the still turbulent country. The dark clouds of political unrest were not dispelled until another army leader, Generalissimo Har-em-hāb, who had lived in Memphis without ever participating in the religious movement, seized the reins of government and the royal crown. The heresy of El Amarneh was ruthlessly stamped out with the same fanaticism as raged during Akh-en-Aten's persecution of the old gods. His name and images were erased from the monuments; he and his successors were completely removed from the list of kings. Posterity learned to know him as the "abominable sinner of El Amarneh," and was told how "the criminal who had laid hands upon Amūn was brought down, and the house of him who had attacked him (Amūn) lay in darkness." And thus El Amarneh has lain deserted under cover of sand . . . until modern archaeology at long last redeemed it from oblivion and revealed its ancient glory.

New Kingdom

1350-1085 B.C.

XIX Dynasty 1350–1200 B.C.
XX Dynasty 1200–1085 B.C.

VI

RAAMSES
AND
THEBES

With Har-em-hāb, the king general, there begins another line of pharaohs whom historians classify into two groups: the Nineteenth and the Twentieth Dynasties. Har-em-hāb, though not their royal ancestor in the true sense of the word, must nevertheless be considered as the founding father since it was he who restored the old order. The figure of this outstanding ruler is known from a portrait-statue made when he was not yet king but still officiating in Memphis as "Hereditary prince, Fan-Bearer on the King's Right, Chief-General and Royal Scribe." It is a life-sized sculpture which once stood in the great Ptah Temple of Memphis, and is now in the Metropolitan Museum of New York.

Har-em-hāb is represented not as a soldier but as an official, a "scribe" sitting with legs crossed, in the attire of a well-to-do gentleman of the late Eighteenth Dynasty. Herbert E. Winlock describes him as "intellectual—even effeminate—with his delicate boyish features and his full, slack torso. . . He has unrolled a scroll of papyrus across his lap and placed his ink-shell upon his knee. His left hand grasps the roll and in his right he holds the pen with which he has just been writing. His task is finished, but he still sits with back bent over it in reverie. A Buddha-like contemplation pervades him, but so instinct with life is his repose that the dead granite has become the almost breathing embodiment of an Egyptian. As a scribe it was fitting to him that he should be composing a psalm to Thoth, the letter-writer of the gods and the divine protector whose influence obtained promotion for all who fol-

122

lowed the clerkly career on earth." His verses praising his influential patron disclose that it is Thoth "who guides him who is in error, recalls every forgotten thing and, knowing the divine mysteries, sets forth their words for his faithful devotees."

As king, Har-em-hāb re-established administrative order through stern measures. All efforts were made "to restore the laws, to prevent injustice, to drive out sin, and to expunge untruth." He disciplined the disorganized army and abolished abuses, without neglecting the welfare of his troops whose pay was increased and whose terms of service were shortened. The men in his personal service received special rewards: "The king called every soldier by his name. They came forth, rejoicing, laden with the provision of the royal house; there was none who had had nothing. Their voice reached heaven, praising all benefactions (from) the heart of all the soldiers of the army."

The priesthoods of Thebes who had abominated the sanctuary of heresy, the Aten Temple of Karnak, were greatly satisfied to see it destroyed and its broken stones used for the two large pylons built by Har-em-hāb on the processional road to the temple of the goddess Mūt.

Har-em-hāb was too much of a self-made man and astute politician to make the same ambitious mistake as General Eye, namely, to legitimize his rights to the throne by marrying a princess of the old dynasty in compliance with traditional law. Perhaps he was afraid of compromising himself and of arousing the suspicion that he had not completely broken with the heretic royal family. Therefore, when he died, after a reign of about thirty-five years, and was buried in a beautiful rock-tomb in the old royal necropolis of Biban el Muluk, there was no legitimate successor to the throne.

Once more, probably so designated by Har-em-hāb, a general of non-royal origin became king. This new

pharaoh was Ramesses, the "Commander-in-chief of the Lord of the Two Lands." As "High Priest of all gods, Deputy of His Majesty in Upper and Lower Egypt, Vizier and Supreme Judge," he had filled the most prominent offices of state. He was the real progenitor of the Nineteenth Dynasty under which Egypt enjoyed another period of great happiness.

The reign of Ramesses I, however, was of short duration. It seems to have lasted no longer than one year. He was followed by his son, Sethy, who turned to a task already begun by Har-em-hāb. By the end of the Eighteenth Dynasty, Egyptian rule in Asia had weakened considerably; Har-em-hāb had attempted to reinforce it and to establish anew the empire of Thut-mose III. After several victorious campaigns, Sethy finally succeeded in restoring the old order at least in Palestine and in subduing the rebellious city princes. In order to facilitate a more efficient surveillance over the reconquered lands, he decided to move his residence from Thebes to Lower Egypt. Tanis, the site of the old Hyksos fortress Avaris at the eastern borders of the Delta, was newly founded and equipped with all splendor, especially by Ramesses II. It was hence renamed "House of Ramesses," or briefly "Ramesses." By this name (Raamses) the city is also mentioned in the Bible (Exodus I, 11), which relates that the oppressed Israelites, forced to statute labor, "built for Pharaoh treasure cities, Pithom and Raamses."

Contemporary court poets gave unbounded praise to the beauty of the new city. The British Egyptologist Alan H. Gardiner once translated some of their verses as follows:

> "How happy is a day of thy (i.e., Pharaoh's) period, how sweet is thy voice when speaking, seeing that thou didst build 'House of Ramesses,' the forefront of every foreign land, the end of Egypt, the city of beauteous balconies, dazzling with halls of azure and emerald, the marshaling place of thy cavalry, the rallying point of thy soldiers, the harbourage of thy ships' troops. . . It is full of food and provisions. It is like to Hermonthis in Upper Egypt (the old neighbor city of Thebes), its duration is like that of Memphis. Everyone hath left his town and settled within its territory. Its western part is the house of Amūn, its southern part the house of Seth. Astarte is in its eastern, and Buto (the patron goddess of Lower Egypt) in its western part. (These verses show that the city was situated between the principal towns of Egypt and Syria.) The citadel that is in it is like the horizon of heaven. Ramesses is in it as god. . . The land goes down to his place. . ."

124

The location of the city of Ramesses was obviously chosen because it was the center of the Egyptian empire that embraced Palestine and Syria in the north and Nubia-Kush in the south.

The old capital of Thebes naturally had to yield some of its political importance to the new "House of Ramesses." Even so, it continued as the main Royal City; and Karnak, the most prominent place of worship in the land. The Temple of Amen-Rē, called by the Egyptians "Ipt-iswet" or "The Counted of the Places," remained the national sanctuary about whose enlargement and embellishment the kings of the Nineteenth and Twentieth Dynasties were no less concerned than their predecessors. Its gigantic Hypostyle Hall, built by Sethy and Ramesses II, is one of the chief wonders of Egyptian architecture. Three hundred and thirty-eight feet in width and one hundred and seventy feet deep, its area covers 54,000 square feet—a space large enough to accommodate the entire cathedral of Notre Dame. The roof was supported by one hundred and thirty-four columns arranged in sixteen rows. Two central rows and two side rows form three naves, of a height of about seventy-nine feet, with six lower aisles adjacent on either side.

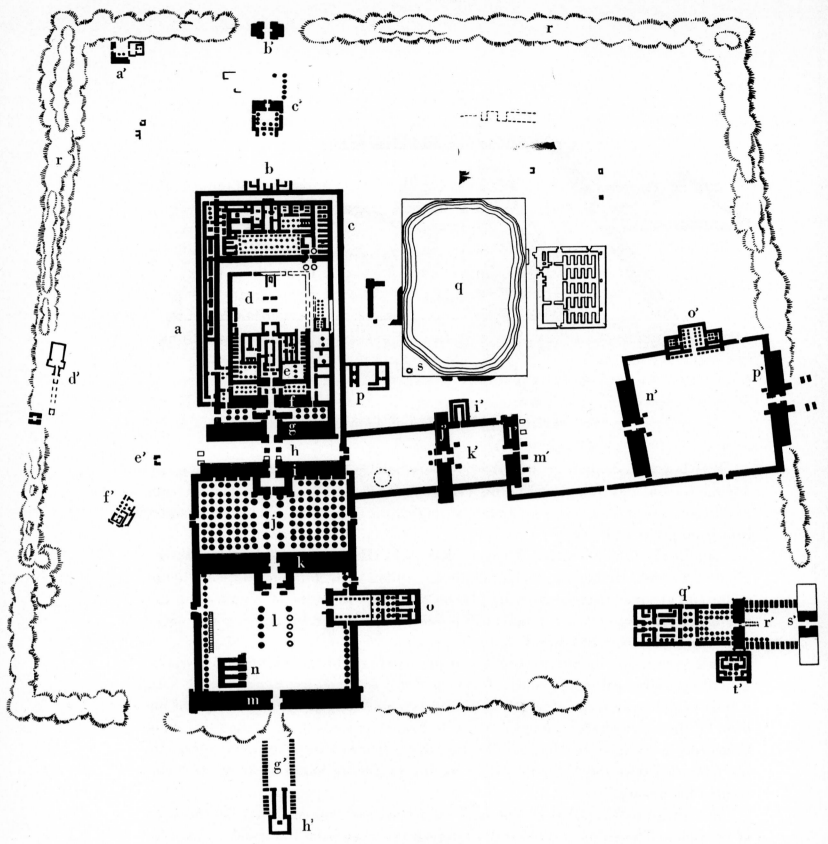

GREAT TEMPLE OF AMŪN. KARNAK

a Great Temple of Amūn
b Mortuary Temple of Thut-mose III
c Great Festal Temple of Thut-mose III
d Remains of Temple of the Middle Empire
e Sixth Pylon
f Fifth Pylon
g Fourth Pylon
h Central Court
i Third Pylon
j Great Hypostyle Hall
k Second Pylon
l Great Court
m First Pylon
n Temple of Sethy II

o Temple of Ramesses III
p Building of Taharka
q Sacred Lake
r Girdle Wall
s Scarabaeus of Amen-hotpe III

a' Temple of Osiris
b' East Gate
c' Small Temple of Ramesses II
d' Temple of Ptah
e' Gate of Ramesses III
f' Sanctuaries of the late Period
g' Avenue of Rams
h' Obelisk of Sethy II

i' Chapel of Thut-mose III
j' Seventh Pylon
k' Statues of Thut-mose III
l' Eighth Pylon
m' Statues of Kings
n' Ninth Pylon
o' Temple of Amen-hotpe II
p' Tenth Pylon
q' Temple of Khonsu
r' Sphinxes of Ramesses XII
s' Portal of Euergetes I
t' Temple of Osiris and Epet

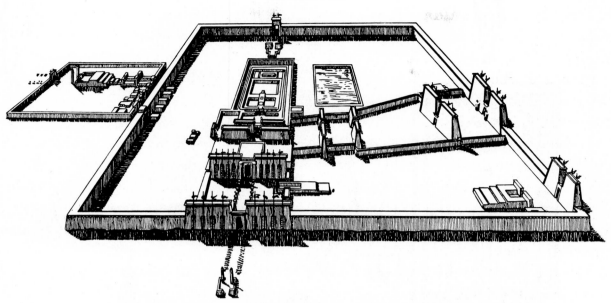

GREAT TEMPLE OF AMŪN. KARNAK (RECONSTRUCTION)

Words are inadequate to describe the overwhelming impression experienced by anyone for the first time entering this veritable forest of columns as he passes from row to row, faced on all sides by figures of mighty kings and gods gazing down upon him from pillar and wall.

The head of the Twentieth Dynasty, Ramesses III, contributed his share to the glory of Karnak. He built a special temple for Amūn, with columned hall and hypostyle; and at some distance from it, a larger sanctuary in honor of Amūn's son, the moon-god Khonsu. A processional road bordered by rows of reclining rams, images of Amūn, leads from this temple to Luxor.

In Luxor itself, Ramesses II enlarged the sanctuary of the Eighteenth Dynasty by adding a large columned court. He adorned this with statues of himself and with a massive pylon, in front of which he placed two obelisks and colossal images of his own. Of these two obelisks, one was taken to France and has stood in the Place de la Concorde in Paris since 1836, while the other remained in its original place. Its inscriptions praise the pharaoh for his having so greatly honored Amen-Rē "who created his beauty."

In contrast to this rather monotonous eulogy are the dynamic reliefs on the walls of the pylon. These depict historically interesting scenes from Ramesses' campaigns against the Hittites: the king in council of war with his princes and generals; the enemy attack against the Egyptian camp fortified by the shields of soldiers; the royal

127

chariot dashing forward while the king directs his arrows against the surrounding enemy; the battlefield littered with dead and wounded, and Hittites fleeing in wild disorder; and the moated fortress of Kadesh with its defenders on the battlements.

Royal Thebes, above all, remained the place to which the kings returned for their final rest. The rock-tombs of Sethy I, Ramesses II and III as well as those of the later Ramessides, in the secluded valley of Biban el Muluk, may be classified among the most impressive monuments ever created by the hand of man in Egypt. Nor must there be overlooked the mortuary temples that fringe the desert: the Temple of Sethy I, the Ramesseum of Ramesses II, and the Medinet Habu Temple of Ramesses III. In bygone days, their halls and courts reverberated with the chanting of priests who went there to make offerings in the sanctum sanctorum. But they were also the scene of secular splendor whenever festivals were celebrated, for each of these sanctuaries was connected with a royal palace. Every year, the pharaoh and his court, including the women of the harem, left the residence at Ramesses to tarry there for a few weeks. From the palace balcony, the so-called "Window of Appearances," he reviewed the festive processions of the priesthood, the athletic games of the soldiery, and the military parades in which prisoners of war were flaunted before His Majesty.

During the intervening century between the death of Thut-mose III and the accession of Har-em-hāb, the Egyptian empire was happily blessed with almost uninterrupted peace. Its dominating position in the Near East was uncontested. But as Akh-en-Aten whiled away precious time in the quiet of his fairy palace of El Amarneh, believing and making believe that the outer world followed its desired course, the storm clouds were gathering in the North. No doubt, the Asiatic kings continued to emphasize their friendship to the pharaoh in reassuring brotherly letters; no doubt, royal trade flourished as monopolies do, and wealth accumulated all along the Nile. Yet "the gods turned their backs on the land," and the Egyptian soldiers supposed to protect the Syrian borders "could do nothing." Even the overwhelming victory of Sethy I in Palestine and his defeat of the Hittites could not fend off threatening danger forever.

Soon after Ramesses II had ascended the throne, he saw himself confronted with the necessity of carrying war once more to the Hittites. Their king had entered into an alliance to drive the Egyptians out of Syria and thus to overthrow once and for all the overlordship of the pharaohs. From all countries "to the ends of the sea," he gathered an army of twenty-five or thirty thousand men, a rather considerable force in those days. He had "foot soldiers and charioteers in large, unheard-of numbers; they covered hills and dales and were as countless as locusts." The Hittite king had

128

taken all the silver he had in his land and "left nothing to remain in order to satisfy his allies and to pay for their troops."

Ramesses, in full realization of the extreme danger, met his enemy with an extraordinarily large contingent of troops on his side. The mighty battle, waged in the vicinity of Kadesh on the Orontes, is minutely described in Egyptian texts and admirably illustrated in reliefs on temple walls.

This decisive event was also glorified by an Egyptian "poet" who composed a voluminous "epos" dealing rather freely with actual facts in order to idolize the pharaoh. He narrates how the host of Egyptians marched northward through the valley of the Orontes river between the mountains of the Lebanon without meeting any resistance from the enemy. Nobody knew the position of the Hittite army. Hired spies reported no danger and declared the Hittite king to be still far away in the North. Thus Ramesses moved unafraid toward Kadesh where he put up a fortified camp. In reality, as the poet goes on to relate, the "wretched prince of the Hittites lay close by in hiding and all ready for battle though afraid to meet His Majesty in combat."

While the Egyptian vanguard marched ahead "unaware and unprepared for an attack," the Hittites suddenly charged and broke into the royal camp. "The men and charioteers faltered before them." When Ramesses was advised of the precarious situation, "he seized his royal headgear, donned his armor, and stepped forth (from his tent) like Mont, the god of war. He dashed forward on his chariot and penetrated the enemy's army all by himself and without any aid. When he looked around, he realized that he was surrounded by countless hostile chariots. . . His foot soldiers and his charioteers had deserted him; there was none to stand his ground and fight."

In his distress, the king prayed to Amūn: "My father, Amūn, have you forsaken your son who did nothing but what you commanded him to do? Did I not build for you many monuments, and give you offerings and all in your temple? What is the meaning of these Asiatics? Now, I am calling upon you, Amūn: I am amidst the barbarians whom I know not; I am all alone, and

nobody is with me. My soldiers have deserted me, and none of my charioteers has even looked back after me. As I call for them, nobody hears me. Yet I know, Amūn is worth more to me than millions of men afoot, than hundred thousands of charioteers, than ten thousand or more brothers and sons. Man's work is naught. Amūn is far better. I do pray from the ends of the world, but my voice carries to Thebes. Amūn hears my call and comes forth. He extends his hand to me; I rejoice when he calls to me: 'Onward! Onward! I am with you, I, your father, the Lord of Victory!' "

Thus Amūn actually answers the pharaoh in his distress. The king's courage is renewed; his heart swells with joy. Like the war-god Mont he shoots to the right and fights to the left. Like Baal he rages. The two thousand five hundred chariots which had encircled him lie shattered before his steeds. None of his enemies is able to fight on. Their hearts are feeble from fear, and their arms weak. They cannot shoot their arrows and have no courage to take to their spears. Like crocodiles he lets them plunge, one atop the other, into the water. None is able to look back. He who falls has no chance to get up again. The enemy is in utter despair. One calls to the other: "This is not an (ordinary) man amongst us; there is a god in his limbs. What he does is not a human deed. Never before has one man alone slain hundreds of thousands. Hasten that we may escape him and save our lives!"

Once more the Egyptian soldiers gather around their heroic king. He reprimands them for their cowardice and reminds them of the good he has done for them. The crime they have committed is beyond words. Even his own faithful charioteer had lost courage.

The following day the battle is continued until the enemy surrenders and "kisses the soil before the pharaoh." The "wretched" prince of the Hittites ceases resistance and writes a letter begging for mercy: "Yesterday you killed hundreds of thousands, and today you return to leave us not a single heir. Be not too severe with us, valorous pharaoh. To be meek is better than to fight."

Ramesses gathers the leaders of his army around him and communicates the letter to them. Their answer is: "Meekness is beautiful; peacefulness must never be reproached."

Hostilities come to an end. The pharaoh offers the hand of peace and returns happily to Ramesses to rest in his palace like the sun-god on his throne.

In spite of its many "poetic licences," this enthusiastic epic of the "Battle of Kadesh" reveals the bare facts. The pharaoh, by his personal courage, turned the initial defeat of his ambushed army into victory, but was unable to exploit it further and to take the fortress of Kadesh. Ramesses had to return to Egypt and be content

133

with an armistice, which is quite a different story from that of the "unconditional surrender" of the poet's fiction.

The state of war between the two powers continued without any definite armed decision for at least another decade. Egypt as well as the Hittite kingdom finally realized the futility of their mutual attempts at conquest. Consequently, a peace treaty was concluded in 1278 B.C. This determined the territorial rights of both powers, at the same time dividing the lands of Syria into two distinct spheres of interest. Peace and understanding were to rule forevermore. Besides being a non-aggression pact, the treaty stipulated mutual assistance against all enemies, foreign and domestic. Its contents are known in detail for its Egyptian text, written in hieroglyphs, was carved into a wall of the Great Temple of Karnak. A slightly varying form of the same document, on cuneiform tablets in the Accadian (Babylonian) language, was found along with the state archives of Boghaskioi in the ruins of the Hittite capital.

The alliance endured, and it was further strengthened by matrimonial ties. Ramesses married a Hittite princess who was taken into his harem not as a subordinate spouse but as official queen under the title "Great Royal Wife, Mistress of the Two Lands."

Peaceful relations also cemented trade and commerce between the two kingdoms. The caravan roads were so secured against highway robbery that an Egyptian inscription could rightfully boast: "Man or woman going on business to Syria may travel without fear to the land of the Hittites, thanks to the great victory of His Majesty."

Upon the death of Ramesses II in 1225 B.C., his then sixty-year-old son Mer-en-Ptah ascended the throne. The fifth year of his reign was marked by an outstanding event of war—a war whose theater was the western border of Egypt. Its historical importance rests on the fact that it was the very first clash of the Egyptian people with Europeans on African soil. The attackers consisted of Libyan tribes, presumably ancestors of the present natives of Tripoli, Tunis, and Algiers. They were joined, however, by diverse sea-peoples from the eastern Mediterranean region who had been attracted by the chances for rich booty. Their names—Shardana, Shakalash, Tursha—permit the assumption that they were related to the Sardinians, Siculers (Sicilians), and Etruscans (Tyrians).

With incipient success they invaded Egypt. "Behold, His Majesty was enraged like a lion." In all haste he gathered his troops and defeated the hostile hordes decisively in a sanguinary battle. The leader of the Libyan forces was put to flight,

135

and—if the Egyptian victory report is to be trusted—"there were thousands of the enemy slain, more than nine thousand taken prisoner, among them the women and children of the Libyan King."

Frequently Mer-en-Ptah has been taken to be the pharaoh under whom the exodus of the Israelites occurred, and "who with all his chariots was overwhelmed in the Red Sea." This hypothesis, however, is founded upon historical quicksand. It rests solely on the premise that Mer-en-Ptah's predecessor, Ramesses, was the pharaoh of the "oppression" who presumably forced the Israelites into labor during the building of the store-cities of Pithom and Raamses. There is no longer any doubt as to the real circumstances of his death. He was not drowned in the waters of the Red Sea, but died in his palace of coronary arterio-sclerosis as was definitely established by medical examination of his mummy found in the necropolis of Thebes.

Furthermore, in the days of Mer-en-Ptah's reign part of the Israelites had already settled in Palestine. One of Mer-en-Ptah's victory inscriptions makes special mention of Israel—incidentally, the only reference to it in Egyptian records—among the known tribes of conquered Palestine: "Canaan is captured; Ascalon is carried captive; Gezer is taken; Yenoam is brought to naught; *Israel* is destroyed, its seed is not; Syria is become as the widows of Egypt; all the lands together are in peace."

Concerning the exodus as well as the migration of the Israelites, the tradition of the Bible may best be taken for what it is: a reminiscence of historical events become legendary, but beyond actual verification in Egyptian annals.

Mer-en-Ptah's death and the ensuing quarrels of succession plunged Egypt into grave domestic difficulties. The throne was constantly being seized by usurpers until Sethy II, a member of the old royal family finally became king and restored internal peace. However, the country was soon again to be shaken by a revolution, about which a document of Ramesses III reports rather darkly: "There came kingless years; a Syrian, by the name of Ersu, seized the government and made the whole country tributary. He and his ilk united themselves in pillaging property. God and man were treated alike. There were no longer offerings brought to the temples."

From this dismal condition, the land was freed by a man named Sethnakht about whose origin nothing definite is known. He restored order, "killed the rebels and cleansed the great throne of Egypt as ruler of the Two Lands." Sethnakht, in fact, became the founder of a new Dynasty—the Twentieth—whose most outstanding representative was his son and successor, Ramesses III.

Attacks from all sides threatened Egypt. In the west, the Libyans had again invaded the land and occupied the cities from the western Delta to Memphis. "Their

warriors thought of inebriating themselves to their heart's desire." But the pharaoh brought their schemes to naught. With a gigantic array of troops, in the main a foreign *soldatesca,* he advanced against the enemy and defeated him. The dead numbered twelve thousand five hundred and thirty-three, and countless prisoners were taken." They lay in their blood as piles of corpses; . . . those whom the sword had spared the king drove captive and bound like birds before his horses; Their women and their children were counted by tens of thousands, and their cattle by hundreds of thousands."

The danger of foreign invasion nevertheless persisted. A few years later, the Libyans made a renewed attempt to gain foothold in the valley of the Nile, but this time failed completely and finally. They were repulsed with great losses, and the captives were settled in fortified camps under special leaders.

A still harder battle awaited Ramesses in the north. From the direction of Syria, a great wave of migrating peoples swept toward Egypt. They had already engulfed the Hittite kingdom and poured into the Syrian states. By sea and by land, in ships and in ox-carts, with women and children, the strangers advanced. "They came, with a flame of fire ahead of them, forward to Egypt. . . They were united, and they laid their hands upon the Two Lands as far as the Circle of the Earth. Their hearts were confident and sated with their plans." The wave met with strong resistance from the Egyptians and finally broke against the pharaoh's superior fleet and army. His victory reports tell how "those who came by land were annihilated, and those who had penetrated into the mouths of the Nile were caught like so many birds in a net."

The invasion of the sea-peoples ended ignominiously. Once more, pharaonic power lived up to its traditional glory; this time not in battle against an organized army like that of the Hittites, but against roaming barbarians and freebooters of the seas. A few tribes of the foreigners settled in Syria; for example, the Peleste and the Zakkar who occupied the coastal district. The Peleste were the people who, known in the Old Testament as the Philistines, gave Palestine its name.

The later years of the reign of Ramesses III were peaceful. In his own words he summed up his benefactions to the country as follows: "I planted the whole land with trees and verdure, and I made the people dwell in their shade. I made Egypt the place the women desired, for no strangers nor any others molested them on the roads. I made the foot-soldiers and the charioteers dwell at home in my day. The mercenaries could stay in their towns and lie full length on their backs; they had no fear, for there was no enemy in Ethiopia (Kush), nor a foe in Syria. Their bows

138

and their weapons reposed in the storehouses while they were satisfied and drunk with joy. Their wives were with them, and their children at their side. They did not need look (furtively) behind themselves; their hearts were confident, for I was their defender and protector. I enlivened the whole land, whether foreigners, common-folk, citizens or people, male or female. I took man out of his misfortune and gave him breath. I rescued from his oppressor him who was of more account than he. I set up each man in the security of his town. I sustained the life of others in the hall of justice. I supplied the land in places where it had been laid waste. The country was well-satisfied during my reign. I did good to the gods as well as to man, and I had nothing that belonged to other people." And addressing himself directly to his subjects, he concluded: "Ye were well-pleasing to my heart, for ye did excel-lently, and ye were zealous for my commands and my commissions."

Even so, the days of his government were not fully as happy as he tried to make the world believe. Repeated wars, extensive and expensive temple buildings, and, last but not least, the gifts he lavished upon the sanctuaries of the land, exhausted the royal exchequer. In proportion to the ever-growing wealth of the various temples whose storehouses and cattle barns were filled to overflowing and their increasing treasures in gold, the royal silos and chests became depleted. It frequently happened in Thebes that the hungry laborers could not be paid the grain that was their due wage. They rebelled and had to strike in order to receive what they had slaved for in endless drudgery. Discontent seized even the palace. A conspiracy was plotted to kill the pharaoh and to replace him by a morganatic son. It was fomented in the royal harem with high officials and officers of the army participating. Commanders of troops garrisoned in Nubia were ready to force the issue by military interference. Even magic was not disdained. Waxen puppets, smuggled into the palace, were in-tended to paralyze its tenants and to create disorder. However, the entire scheme was only partly successful. The pharaoh was assassinated, but the conspirators were arrested and haled before a special court of justice.

The dead king who already resided with Osiris, the Lord of Eternity—in actu-ality his as yet uncrowned successor—instructed the investigating commissions as to the desired legal proceedings. The protocols concerning this case of high treason, its course and final outcome, have been preserved. The guilty were convicted. Death sentences were pronounced, which the most prominent personages among the crim-inals were permitted to carry out themselves. In other words, they were granted the privilege of committing suicide, while the rest were publicly executed. Minor culprits escaped with ears and noses cut off.

140

The earthly remains of the murdered king were taken to Thebes. His burial in a rock-tomb in the Valley of the Kings was preceded by solemn funeral services in the mortuary temple of Medinet Habu.

On this occasion, an extensive report concerning the king's government was publicly read. Accounting in detail for all his deeds and donations to the temples, it supposedly emanated from the lips of the late pharaoh but was actually composed by his successor. This strange document, the largest of all known papyrus rolls, is now in the possession of the British Museum. The king concluded his report with a prayer for his son Ramesses IV, "begotten by Amūn, Atum and Ptah, and destined to be his successor": "Amūn has decreed to him his reign upon earth; he has doubled him his lifetime greater than any king's." And his subjects are admonished in these words: "Be ye attached to his sandals, kiss the earth in his presence, bow down to him, follow him at all times, adore him, praise him, magnify his beauty as ye do to the sun-god every morning . . . that ye may enjoy his favor, in possession of his provision every day."

Historical data on Ramesses IV and his seven successors, all of whom bear the name Ramesses, is rather meager. Like Ramesses III before them, they tried to emulate the greater Ramesses II, but none of them was equal to his personality. The last of the line, Ramesses XI, is also the last of the pharaohs to build himself a rock-tomb in the royal necropolis of Thebes. Under him faded the splendor of the New Kingdom which had so brilliantly illumined the world of the Near East during the Eighteenth and Nineteenth Dynasties. Egypt's might had reached the days of decline.

Late Period

1085-525 B.C.

XXI Dynasty 1085–945
XXII Dynasty 945–745
XXIII–XXIV Dynasty 745–712
XXV Dynasty 712–663
XXVI Dynasty 663–525

VII

TANIS
AND
SAIS

As the political strength of the Ramessides waned, the power of the clergy in Thebes grew, finally becoming a state within the state. Decisions in all matters of public importance were made in the Great Temple of Amūn, the king of gods whose will was mysteriously made known by the High Priest upon the occasion of festal processions.

The actual powers of government, however, rested in the hands of the army, particularly the Upper Egyptian contingent which was commanded by the viceroy of Kush. Thus when under Ramesses XI a rebellion started in Thebes, the military authorities invested an officer named Hrihor with the office of High-Priest of Amūn. Soon after, he became viceroy of Kush and general-in-chief, and took over one of the two highest administrative posts: the vizierate of Thebes. With hierarchical, military, and political powers in hand, he found it easy to push the impotent pharaoh into the background and, undoubtedly by consent of the divine oracle of Thebes, to invest himself with the crown. He was nevertheless not strong enough to extend his supremacy over Lower Egypt. The vizier of the northern half of the land and commander of the Lower Egyptian troops, who resided in Ramesses-Tanis, controlled this section of the kingdom. Since he, too, pronounced himself King of Upper and Lower Egypt, the empire was threatened with secession. Once more the danger of an exhausting civil war was imminent.

150

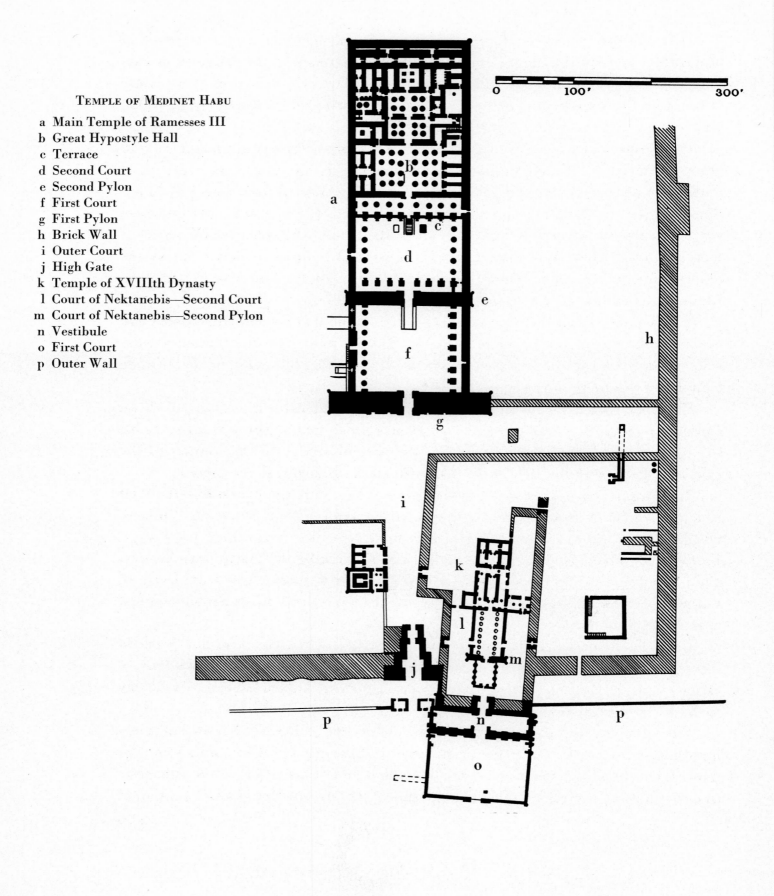

TEMPLE OF MEDINET HABU

a Main Temple of Ramesses III
b Great Hypostyle Hall
c Terrace
d Second Court
e Second Pylon
f First Court
g First Pylon
h Brick Wall
i Outer Court
j High Gate
k Temple of XVIIIth Dynasty
l Court of Nektanebis—Second Court
m Court of Nektanebis—Second Pylon
n Vestibule
o First Court
p Outer Wall

0   100'   300'

The political astuteness of the Amūn priesthood, however, found a means of preventing the fatal cleavage. They arranged for a marriage of the daughter of Psusennes, the second king of the Tanis (Twenty-first) Dynasty, to a scion of the house of the High Priests, who forthwith became the legitimate heir to the Lower Egyptian kingdom.

The hundred and forty-five years of the Twenty-first Dynasty are historically of minor importance. While Nubia-Kush remained with the empire as a province, Palestine, no longer under pharaonic rule since the invasion of the sea-peoples under Ramesses III, was definitely lost as Egyptian territory. The pharaohs, before whose very name the Syrian princes had once bowed their humble heads, were deprived of their influence. How little the pharaonic name meant abroad is borne out by the report made by a traveling temple official of Thebes. This account of a certain Wen-Amūn by name may be retold here in abridged form:

It so happened that the processional bark of Amūn had become dilapidated and needed replacement. The problem was how to get the money for the necessary cedar wood from Byblos in the Lebanon. It was finally supplied by taking up a collection from those who were in power in Upper Egypt.

Equipped with letters of recommendation Wen-Amūn made his voyage as official emissary to King Smendes in Tanis, and thence proceeded by sea to Byblos. As his ship put in at the port of Dor (south of the present Haifa) in the country of the Zakkar, a member of his crew absconded with all the gold and silver aboard.

Wen-Amūn addressed himself to the prince of Dor with the request that the thief be apprehended in order to recover the stolen currency. The prince kindly obliged, but the search was to no avail. Wen-Amūn finally decided to continue his voyage. En route, however, he made the rather rash step of taking the matter into his own hands. He relieved a party of Zakkar people—chance acquaintances from Dor—of a satchel of gold, simply declaring that he would keep it until the stolen moneys had been restored to him.

Upon his ultimate arrival in Byblos, the prince of the city who had been informed of the whole incident told Wen-Amūn that he was unwilling to risk complications with the Zakkar. "Make haste," he said to Wen-Amūn, "and get out of my harbor!"

The following day, the Egyptian is haled before the prince and has an extremely humiliating interview. The prince asks rather indignantly for Wen-Amūn's credentials. When the Egyptian is forced to confess that he left his letters of recommendation in Tanis, he is bluntly called an impostor. After all, how could any Egyptian of

153

rank make a trading trip as miserably equipped as Wen-Amūn? Of course the prince's ancestors had carried out orders from Egypt, but in their day the pharaoh had sent six ships replete with merchandise. And with a sneer, he adds: "I am not your servant, nor the servant of him who sent you (the High Priest of Amūn)."

Wen-Amūn answers in words ringing with pride that Amūn is still the lord and master of the world. "There is no ship upon the waters that belongs not to him. His is the sea; his the Lebanon; and you too are his servant."

The prince of Byblos capitulates. They agree upon sending a messenger back to Tanis with the request that the wherewithal be advanced. In due time, gold and silver mugs, fine linens, papyrus, and other valuables arrive; the prince issues orders to cut the desired timber and to transport it to port. Wen-Amūn's promise to pay the balance upon his return to Thebes settles the matter to mutual satisfaction. The Egyptian emissary could have set sail for home. Suddenly, however, ships of the Zakkar appear in the harbor to take Wen-Amūn prisoner for his alleged theft.

The prince of Byblos frustrates the scheme, and Wen-Amūn is permitted to depart. After some additional incidents—the end of his report is unfortunately not preserved—he happily reaches Tanis and finally Thebes.

There is no question but that an Egyptian official sent abroad by the High Priest of Amūn in the time of Sesostris or Thut-mose would have been quite differently treated by a Syrian "barbarian." The disrespect Wen-Amūn encountered tells eloquently of the growing weakness that had become Egypt's lot.

The final fate of the Twenty-first Dynasty, founded by King Smendes is unknown. About 945 B.C., Sheshonq, the leader of a Libyan army, succeeded in securing royal sovereignty from the city of Bubastis over the whole of Egypt. Following the old tradition, he legitimized his house's claims to the throne of the pharaohs by marrying his son to a daughter of the old dynasty. The residence remained in Tanis, where a decade ago French excavators discovered the untouched tomb of King Psusennes and the considerably damaged graves of several rulers of the Twenty-second Dynasty.

King Sheshonq is identical with King Shishak (Susakim) who, according to the Bible (Second Chronicles: 12, 2), in the fifth year of King Rehoboam of Judah "came up against Jerusalem and took away the treasures of the house of the Lord, and the treasures of the King's house; he carried away also the shields of gold which Solomon had made."

On a wall of the Great Temple of Karnak, Sheshonq immortalized this Palestinian campaign—though after all of no actual political advantage for Egypt—

155

listing all the cities he claimed to have conquered, many of which bear familiar names.

While the rather unimportant successor of Sheshonq ruled in Egypt, an independent Ethiopian kingdom in faraway Nubia arose about the middle of the eighth century. Its beginnings are shrouded in historical darkness. Possibly a scion of the High Priests of Thebes, who in the capacity of a viceroy of Kush administered the southern lands and commanded the Upper Egyptian army, shook off Egyptian sovereignty and assumed kingship. It is no less possible that a native Nubian house realized the weakness of the mother country and set up a kingdom of its own.

The capital of the Ethiopian state became Napata, a main city of the Amūn cult even during the Eighteenth Dynasty and regarded as a second Holy Thebes. In its vicinity, the Harvard-Boston Expedition discovered the small stone pyramids which are the oldest tombs of Ethiopian kings.

The Ethiopian state aspired to become the exemplar of a Divine Kingdom. Its monarch considered himself the true guardian of Egyptianism, particularly of Egyptian religion and the Amūn faith, and hence claimed legitimate rulership over the entire country. He adopted the full titulary of the Egyptian pharaohs and proudly called himself "King of Upper and Lower Egypt, Lord of the Two Lands."

The Egyptian state, on the other hand, disintegrated more and more. Several of the city princes, supported by their military contingents, attained independence but without gaining any power over districts not their own. Such expansion was finally achieved by Tefnakhte, Prince of Sais, who "occupied the entire West (Lower Egypt)" and had the other "princes and city lords follow him like dogs." When he penetrated into Upper Egypt, however, King Piankhi of the Ethiopians heeded the call of the hard-pressed dynasts and decided to intervene with armed force.

Tefnakhte was defeated and had to sue for peace. His son Bocchoris made an equally unsuccessful attempt to conquer the southland. He too was repulsed by the Ethiopians who in turn finally occupied all of Egypt. From 715 to 633 B.C., the negro kings were seated on the throne of Hor as the Twenty-fifth Dynasty, fully recognized in their overlordship by the petty princes.

While Egypt drained her blood in domestic strife, a new world power arose on the soil of the Near East in the Assyrian empire. Syria and Palestine had already fallen. The Ethiopian kings Shabako and Taharka, supported by Syrian princes including Hirkia of Judah, tried in vain to fend off imminent catastrophe. In 671 B.C. Assyria took Memphis; Thebes, eight years later. With this blow, Egypt was reduced to the status of a province. The Egyptian princes retained their territories as vassals of the

156

Great Kings of Nineveh but had to suffer supervision by an Assyrian army of occupation. Even the mightiest among them, Necho of Sais and Memphis, and his son and successor Psamtik (663-609 B.C.) could not escape the same fate. Later, however, when the Assyrians became involved in a hard struggle in Asia Minor, Psamtik succeeded in shaking off the yoke and in defeating the native dynasts who opposed him in the name of Assyria. Thebes—where the Ethiopians had maintained themselves for a time and real authority was vested in the procurator "Prince" Mentu-em-hēt—was regained by Psamtik through clever politics.

159

THE RESTORATION AND THE END

After three centuries of strife and struggle, Egypt was once more to undergo a happy change of fortune. Under Psamtik and his successors, the kings of the Twenty-sixth Dynasty, Necho, Psamtik II, Apries, and Amasis, the country enjoyed a new, though its last, era of independent prosperity.

Sais, the native town of the ruling house, became the capital and center of life. Though the great milestone at the road's end, Sais from days immemorial had been renowned as cult place of the goddess Neith—"The Great, the Mother of Gods" whom Greece identified with Athene—and also as the locale of numerous myths. Furthermore, it was famed as the seat of a medical school which had been in existence since the third millennium B.C.

Now in the eighth century, for nearly one hundred and fifty years as Egyptian capital, Sais was given the political prominence it had missed. Situated in the western Delta not far distant from the present Rosetta arm of the Nile, it shared the fate of most Lower Egyptian cities. Today, it has disappeared almost completely from the face of the earth. Not a single stone remains of what Herodotos lauded as the "great and marvellous palace" of the Psamtiks and the "marvellous temple" of Neith-Athene; or of its obelisks, huge images, and man-headed sphinxes. Herodotos also admired the royal tombs in the sacred precinct, and attended the mystery plays representing "The God's (Osiris') Sufferings" performed on the holy temple lake at night.

Beside the city of Sais, Memphis retained its old importance as seat of the administration and center of art. The splendor of Thebes was definitely on the wane. A few buildings were added to the Great Temple, but there were no longer any such sumptuous festivals as the pharaohs of the New Kingdom had celebrated. The "Holy City" was relegated to the rank of a mere provincial town. On a visit to Thebes, the hundred-gated, Strabo found only scattered miserable villages where once gleamed "the heaps of precious ingots" praised in the Iliad (IX, 379 ff.).

The new freedom and unity which Psamtik regained for Egypt created a new consciousness of life in her people. At the same time, however, they realized the present period's intrinsic emptiness as well as the threadbareness of its physical ex-

160

terior. From the ruins upon which the state had been built, little confidence was engendered to raise a fresh harvest of culture. The people looked back and tried to extract the vitally needed blood from the roots of the past. The Pyramid Era loomed as the Golden Age, as the time in which Egypt had unfolded her best. And the days of Sesostris and Thut-mose also seemed worthy of emulation. The Ethiopians in Napata had shown the value of antiquity. It was they who had pointed out the road which an unadulterated priestly orthodoxy might take toward the realization of political and spiritual ideals. The trail marked out by the Ethiopians was now followed and broadened.

Ancient, long-forgotten titles were dusted off and applied to offices they no longer befitted. Inscriptions were quaintly styled. On monuments, people appear in ancient garb that was no longer being worn in current life. The old Pyramid Texts were taken and copied on the walls of tombs and coffins, though their language and meaning were only partially or not at all understood. In order to appear as descendants of an exalted ancestry, the kings adopted in their titulary certain appellations which the pharaohs of the Old Kingdom had borne thousands of years ago. Artists as well tended to apply antique forms to their work. Of course there were schools of sculptors who found an independent way of expressing themselves in portraiture. The majority of the wall reliefs either slavishly copied the ancient originals or at best transformed them into a novel "Neo-Memphite" style.

All this should not imply that national romanticism with its trend toward antiquity had no counterpart in efforts to live up to the times. The degree to which the inner structures of the state, administration, finance, and law adapted themselves to changed conditions cannot be exactly determined. In foreign policy, this much is evident: Egypt opened herself much wider to outside influences than in bygone days. New trade connections were established with Greece and her colonies in Asia Minor, and the old commerce with the coastal cities of Phoenicia, especially with Sidon, Tyre, and Byblos, was revived. The ports at the several mouths of the Nile were thrown open to foreign merchant vessels, and aliens began manufacturing at various inland places. Efficient, shrewd Syrian and Greek traders settled in town and country. The benefits derived from their aiding Egypt's economic progress were enjoyed by entirely different classes from those similarly privileged in the New Kingdom. The priesthood was seemingly pushed into the background; the wealth of the temples was depleted. The major part of the revenue was used for the maintenance of a strong army. The alien mercenaries who were instrumental in national reconstruction continued to be the dynasty's firmest domestic support and safeguard against all dangers

167

from without. In addition to the land army, a navy was created primarily for the protection of the merchant fleet but also for strictly military enterprises overseas, such as the conquest of Cyprus by King Amasis.

It was the great misfortune of the new dynasty that it did not content itself with the success of its commercial policies but became intent on designs for world power. Like its predecessors, it toyed with the idea of conquering Palestine and establishing Egyptian hegemony in Syria. Herein lay an invitation to conflict with Babylonia, the heir to the Assyrian empire.

In 605 B.C. Pharaoh Necho suffered a decisive defeat at the hands of the Babylonian King Nebuchadrezzar, of which the Bible says (Second Kings, 24, 7): "and the king of Egypt came not again any more out of his land; for the king of Babylon had taken from the river of Egypt unto the river Euphrates all that pertained to the king of Egypt."

The Babylonians in turn attacked successfully but failed to conquer the land of the Nile. Only after Cyrus, the Persian king, had smashed Babylon and founded an empire of his own, did his son and successor Cambyses deliver the fatal blow against Egypt in 525 B.C. Within a few months the country was conquered; the once proud empire of the pharaohs ended as a satrapy of Persia.

VIII

Egypt after the Persian Conquest
525 B.C. to 1943 A.D.

PTOLEMAIC PERIOD: 332-30

    Center: Alexandria

ROMAN PERIOD: 30 B.C.-395.

    Battle of Actium 30 B.C.: Antony defeated.
    Egypt a Roman province.—Christianity introduced into Egypt
        ca. 150.

BYZANTINE PERIOD: 395-640.

    Partition of the Roman Empire: 395.

THE MIDDLE AGES: 640-1517.

    Egypt a province of the Empire of the Caliphs: 640-969.
    Egypt under independent dynasties.
        (Fatimids, Aiyubids, Mamelukes): 969-1517.

MODERN HISTORY: 1517-1943

    Turkish Domination: 1517-1914

        French Occupation (Napoleon Bonaparte): 1798-1801.
        François Champollion deciphers the Hieroglyphs: 1822.
        Mohammed Alì and his dynasty: since 1805.
        Opening of the Suez Canal: 1869.
        Egypt under British Control (Lord Cromer): 1882-1914.
        The rebellion of the Mahdist in the Sudan (General Gordon
            1885): 1883-1898.

        World War I: Egypt declared as a British Protectorate; The
            "Khedive" Hussein Kamil proclaimed "Sultan of
            Egypt": 1914.—"Sultan" and "King" Fuad: 1917-1936.
            —Egypt proclaimed "kingdom" as an hereditary mon-
            archy: 1923.

        World War II: Since 1939.
            Egypt joins the Allies: 1939.
            The Axis Army (Rommel) conquers North Africa (To-
            bruk) and advances towards Alexandria: 1942 (June).
            Counter-Offensive of Generals Alexander and Montgom-
            ery, *Battle of el-Alamein:* 1942 (August).

172

For the readers' convenience in order to establish a comparative perspective of the various periods in the development of Egyptian history to the corresponding periods of the classical, i.e. Greek and Roman as well as the Western histories, the publisher has reprinted the chart "contemporary" culture epochs from Oswald Spengler's *The Decline of the West* by permission of Alfred A. Knopf, Publisher, New York.

	EGYPTIAN	CLASSICAL	WESTERN

PRE-CULTURAL PERIOD   CHAOS OF PRIMITIVE EXPRESSION FORMS. MYSTICAL SYMBOLISM AND NAIVE IMITATION

EXCITATION	Thinite Period (3400-3000)	Mycenean Age (1700-1600) / Late-Egyptian (Minoan) / Late-Babylonian (Asia Minor)	Merovingian-Carolingian Era (500-900)

CULTURE   LIFE-HISTORY OF A STYLE FORMATIVE OF THE ENTIRE INNER-BEING. FORM-LANGUAGE OF DEEPEST SYMBOLIC NECESSITY

	EGYPTIAN	CLASSICAL	WESTERN
I. EARLY PERIOD (Ornament and architecture as elementary expression of the young world-feeling.) (The "Primitives")			
1. Birth and Rise. Forms sprung from the Land, unconsciously shaped			
	OLD KINGDOM (2900-2400)	DORIC (1100-500)	GOTHIC (900-1500)
	Dynasties IV-V (2930-2625)	11th to 9th Centuries	11th to 13th Centuries
	Geometrical Temple style / Pyramid temples / Ranked plant-columns / Rows of flat-relief / Tomb statues	Timber building / Doric column / Architrave / Geometric (Dipylon) style / Burial urns	Romanesque and Early-Gothic vaulted cathedrals / Flying buttress / Glass painting, Cathedral sculpture
2. Completion of the early form-language. Exhaustion of possibilities. Contradiction			
	VI Dynasty (2625-2574) / Extinction of pyramid-style and epic-idyllic relief style / Floraison of archaic portrait-plastic	8th and 7th Centuries / End of archaic Doric-Etruscan style / Proto-Corinthian–Early-Attic (mythological) vase painting	14th-15th Centuries / Late Gothic and Renaissance / Floraison and waning of fresco and statue. From Giotto (Gothic) to Michelangelo (Baroque). Siena, Nurnberg. The Gothic picture from Van Eyck to Hollbein. Counterpoint and oil-painting
II. LATE PERIOD (Formation of a group of arts urban and conscious, in the hands of individuals.) ("Great Masters")	MIDDLE KINGDOM (2150-1800)	IONIC (650-350)	BAROQUE (1500-1800)
3. Formation of a mature artistry			
	XIth Dynasty. Delicate and telling art (Almost no traces left)	Completion of the temple-body (Peripteros, stone) / The Ionic column / Reign of fresco-painting till Polygnotus (460) / Rise of free plastic "in the round" ("Apollo of Tenea" to Hageladas)	The pictorial style in architecture from Michelangelo to Bernini (d. 1680) / Reign of oil-painting from Titian to Rembrandt (d. 1664) / Rise of music from Orlando Lasso to H. Schutz (d. 1672)

	EGYPTIAN	CLASSICAL	WESTERN

4. Perfection of an intellectualized form-language

EGYPTIAN	CLASSICAL	WESTERN
XIIth Dynasty (2000-1788) Pylon-temple, Labyrinth Character-statuary and historical reliefs	Maturity of Athens (480-350) The Acropolis Reign of Classical plastic from Myron to Phidias End of strict fresco and ceramic paint- ing (Zeuxis)	Rococo Musical architecture ("Rococo") Reign of classical music from Bach to Mozart End of classical oil-painting (Watteau to Goya)

5. Exhaustion of strict creativeness. Dissolution of grand form. End of the Style. "Classicism" and "Romanticism"

EGYPTIAN	CLASSICAL	WESTERN
Confusion after about 1750 (No remains)	The age of Alexander The Corinthian column Lysippus and Apelles	Empire and Biedermeyer Classicist taste in architecture Beethoven, Delacroix

CIVILIZATION EXISTENCE WITHOUT INNER FORM. MEGALOPOLITAN ART AS A COMMONPLACE: LUX-URY, SPORT, NERVE EXCITEMENT. RAPIDLY CHANGING FASHIONS IN ART (REVIVALS, ARBITRARY DISCOVERIES, BORROWINGS)

1. "Modern Art." "Art problems." Attempts to portray or to excite the megalopolitan consciousness. Transformations of music, architecture and painting into mere craft-arts

EGYPTIAN	CLASSICAL	WESTERN
Hyksos Period (Preserved only in Crete; Minoan art)	Hellenism Pergamene Art (theatricality) Hellenistic painting modes (veristic, bi- zarre, subjective) Architectural display in the cities of the Diadochi	19th and 20th Centuries Liszt, Berlioz, Wagner Impressionism from Constable to Leibl and Manet American architecture

2. End of form-development. Meaningless, empty, artificial, pretentious architecture and ornament. Imitation of archaic and exotic motives

EGYPTIAN	CLASSICAL	WESTERN
XVIII Dynasty (1580-1350) Rock temple of Deir el-Bahri. Memmon-Colossi. Art of Cnossos and El Amar-neh	Roman Period (1000-100) Indiscriminate piling of all three orders. Fora, theatres (Colosseum). Triumphal arches	From 2000

3. Finale. Formation of a fixed stock of forms. Imperial display by means of material and mass. Provincial craft-art

EGYPTIAN	CLASSICAL	WESTERN
XIX Dynasty (1350-1205) Gigantic buildings of Luxor, Karnak and Abydos Small-art (beast plastic, textiles, arms)	Trajan to Aurelian Gigantic fora, thermae, colonnades, tri-umphal arches Roman provincial art (ceramic, statu-ary, arms)	

PHOTOGRAPHS

176

177

178

179